When Not to Borrow

Unconventional Financial Wisdom
to Set Your Church Free

Ray Bowman
with **Eddy Hall**

Foreword by H. B. London Jr.

 Baker Books

A Division of Baker Book House Co
Grand Rapids, Michigan 49516

Published by Baker Books
a division of Baker Book House Company
P.O. Box 6287, Grand Rapids, MI 49516-6287

Printed in the United States of America

For information about academic books, resources for Christian leaders, and all new releases available from Baker Book House, visit our web page at http://www.bakerbooks.com.

Library of Congress Cataloging-in-Publication Data
Bowman, Ray
    When not to borrow : unconventional financial wisdom to set your church free / Ray Bowman with Eddy Hall.
    p.   cm.
    Includes bibliographical references.
    ISBN 0-8010-9021-0 (pbk.)
    1. Church finance. I. Hall, Eddy. II. Title
BV770.B63 1996   96-33859
254.8—dc20

To
my wife
and partner,
Sara Denise Bowman,
consultant

Contents

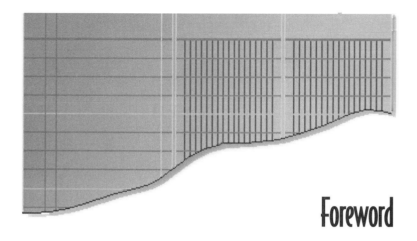

Foreword

When Not to Borrow is a map of a man's heart, a heart that beats with concern for a church seemingly determined to so burden itself with debt that it cannot do justice to its calling. I was a pastor for thirty-one years. One church I pastored built a building and added some fifteen additions over sixteen years without excessive debt. This church was liberated. We were free to take risks, minister creatively, and provide servant/shepherd leadership for all ages.

I also pastored a great church that was hobbled by heavy indebtedness. Though this church was a blessing to lead, our constant battle to service the debt prohibited both aggressive ministry and adequate staffing.

Comparing these two churches, I think of two runners at a starting line. One is excited about the challenge before him, ready for the race. The other, though determined, carries on his back a hundred-pound weight. He will run and probably do as well as anyone can under so heavy a weight. But however great his passion, he will be less successful than he could have been, exert far more energy than he would have needed to, and be at a distinct disadvantage to the other runner.

Much like these runners, some churches have put priority on fiscal responsibility and now enjoy a wonderful freedom for ministry. Others have borrowed beyond their ability to comfortably carry the load. They go forward, but only with great difficulty, as though they are laboring under a massive weight.

Will Ray tell you never to borrow? Certainly not. What he will do, from both experience and personal knowledge, is give you guidance on the whens, hows, and whys of healthy church financing. I am convinced that every pastor should have *When Not to Borrow* in his own library, and every local church should have *When Not to Borrow* attached to the official church board minutes.

I urge you to read this book carefully. Learn from a man who has observed the church at its best—and at its worst. Take counsel from Ray Bowman, a man who wants your church to become all that God has in mind for it to be.

H. B. London Jr.
Vice President
Ministry Outreach/Pastoral Ministries
Focus on the Family

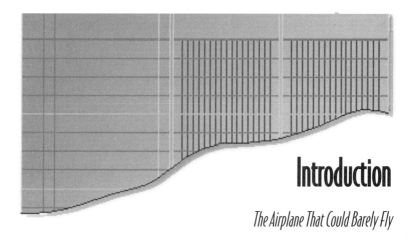

Introduction

The Airplane That Could Barely Fly

For more than forty years I have worked with churches, first as an architect, more recently as a consultant on facilities and finances. I have worked with churches fighting for their financial lives as well as churches enjoying tremendous financial vitality. I have watched churches overcome tremendous financial obstacles to break through to freedom. And I have learned from them all.

One thing I have learned is that almost all the financial problems that afflict churches spring from three underlying causes. The purpose of this book is to show your church practical, proven ways to avoid or overcome these three root problems so you can enjoy the greatest possible financial freedom for ministry.

A simple parable illustrates how these three conditions can endanger the life of the church.

It took a little longer than expected for the plane to reach takeoff speed, and even once it was in the air, the engines labored and the plane did not gain altitude fast enough.

The captain radioed the control tower. "We have a problem here," he announced. "Perhaps a fuel or engine problem. It's all I can do to keep climbing."

The answer from the control tower was intended to reassure. "You don't have a mechanical problem. It's just that you're flying heavy today. Not only is your flight full, but you're carrying about twice as much baggage as usual. We needed to send a lot of unclaimed baggage to our hub office, so we put it all on your flight. Plus you're carrying a couple of good-sized pieces of freight."

The captain felt only sightly comforted as the plane kept laboring to reach flying altitude. Eventually, the plane completed its climb and the captain turned on the autopilot. He looked out over the landscape, scanned his dials, then leaned back and breathed deeply.

Suddenly he jerked forward. That compass reading. Was that right? He rechecked the flight plan he had been given. Yes, it said he should be going northeast. But wasn't his destination northwest?

He radioed the control tower again. "Are you sure this flight plan is right?" he asked. "Shouldn't we be going northwest?"

"Oh, don't worry about it," came the answer. "It's probably okay. If you want us to, next time you're here we'll look over your flight plan."

Not at all reassured this time, the captain checked his map to see what his heading really should be. Sure enough, his heading was off by almost ninety degrees. Each moment in the air was taking him farther from his intended destination.

And that's when he noticed the fuel gauge. Though he had been in the air less than fifteen minutes, he only had enough fuel for another half hour of flight. He made his third call to the control tower. "I must have a major fuel leak," he warned. "I'm already more than three-quarters empty."

"Oh, nothing to worry about," came the reply. "The crew just didn't get around to refueling before you took off."

This story is preposterous, of course. Nothing like this could ever happen. Or could it? The truth is, something very much like this is happening in many churches today.

I believe it is the nature of the church, this body of believers in whom God's Spirit lives, to thrive, just as it is the nature of an airplane to fly. Yet it seems to take all the energy some churches can muster just to stay aloft. Why? Often it is because, like the airplane in the story, they are overloaded, off course, or underfueled—or even all three.

Financial Barrier #1: Overloaded

Like an airplane so heavily loaded that it can hardly get off the ground, many churches are so burdened with debt that they cannot adequately fund the church's present ministries. I've worked with churches that couldn't hire urgently needed staff because they had to pay debt. I've seen scores of churches that were spending little or nothing on intentional outreach, and because of debt, couldn't have invested much in outreach no matter how badly they might have wanted to. I've seen churches so buried in debt that they literally couldn't buy crayons for children's Sunday school.

Even churches not laboring under crushing debt often carry more debt than necessary. In many cases they have come to accept their situation as normal. They can't even imagine how much more they could do if only they were free of debt.

There is a better way. Part 1 of this book shows how your church can throw off the heavy load of indebtedness and enjoy the freedom of operating debt-free—what I call a provision economy. Picking up where our previous book, *When Not to Build*,[1] leaves off, it outlines a proven, workable strategy for getting your church out of debt and keeping it out of debt, even through a major building program. Your church can get out of the borrowing business, greatly enhancing its capacity for ministry.

Financial Barrier #2: Off Course

Of all the church mission statements I've read—and I've read a lot—I have never read a bad one. I've never read a mission statement that says, "We want to be a self-serving church, focusing only on our own needs and ignoring the needs of those around us." Yet a church that would never dream of saying this in its mission statement often says something very close to it in the document that probably more than any other reveals its real priorities—its budget.

When I work with churches on their finances, I go through their budgets line by line looking for any spending I can honestly label as intentional local outreach. Many churches give generously to missions far away, but hardly any designate even 3 percent for intentional outreach in their own communities; most budget less than 1 percent for this purpose.

A church's mission statement is its stated destination. Its budget is like a flight plan. When the flight plan (budget) is not defined by the intended destination (stated mission), the flight plan cannot take the church where it wants to go.

Part 2 of this book, "From Institutionalism to Purpose," shows how your church can use its budget as a tool to measure whether it is on or off course. It spells out how your church can then develop a ministry-focused budget; one shaped not by institutionalism but by your church's stated purpose. You can apply this principle not only to your church's finances but also to the staff's time and the church's use of facilities so that the way it uses all its resources is purpose driven, not institution driven.

Financial Barrier #3: Underfueled

Just as it takes more than a full tank of fuel to get a plane to its destination, money alone cannot make a church thrive. But too little money, like too little fuel, can keep your church from doing what it is called to do.

A church that is not growing can coast along with its members giving about 3 percent of their income. A church whose members are giving 5 to 6 percent of their income can enjoy modest growth. But experience shows that in a church with no debt, members need to give 8 to 12 percent of their income for the church to sustain vigorous growth.

How can a church inspire its people to give generously to a shared vision for ministry without forcing its pastor to be a perennial fundraiser? And how can a church help its members achieve the financial freedom that enables them to give more generously? Part 3 shows how a church can go from insufficiency to plenty.

Freedom for Ministry

No church ever sets out to take on excessive debt. No church likes to say no to opportunities to meet people's needs because mortgage payments are "stealing" funds needed for ministry. No church ever wants its pastor to have to beg for money just to cover basic operating expenses. Yet most churches, to some degree, live with one or more of these financial burdens.

Your church can avoid or overcome the paralyzing effects of indebtedness, institutionalism, and insufficiency and enjoy the freedom for ministry that comes with provision, purpose, and plenty. But it won't happen overnight. The "unconventional financial wisdom" outlined in this book is no quick fix. For most churches this approach to church finances is fundamentally different from any they have followed before. It may take time for the leaders and members of your congregation to adopt these principles as their own.

But even once you set your course, it can take years of generous giving and disciplined budgeting to erase large debts. For a growing church that will eventually build, that generosity and discipline must continue for the church to know the freedom that comes from building without debt.

For a church willing to pay the price, the rewards can be great. A church that embraces these principles and lives by them can enjoy real freedom from the crippling effects of indebtedness, institutionalism, and insufficiency, a degree of freedom to minister that few churches even dream of. If you want to be a part of that kind of church, this unconventional wisdom is for you.

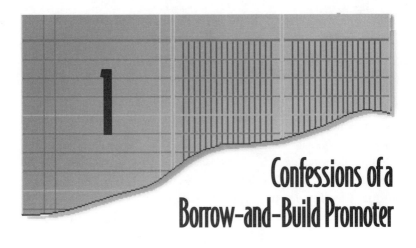

Confessions of a Borrow-and-Build Promoter

A s my wife, Sally, and I entered the thirty-five-hundred-seat sanctuary, the warm voices of gathering worshipers welcomed us. Sparkling Christmas trees, graceful garlands, and the cheerful clamor of musical instruments tuning up heightened our anticipation. Even on an ordinary Sunday, we knew, the music here was excellent. This was Christmas Sunday; today it would be extraordinary.

Though we were visitors, we knew the pastor here. He was among the best preachers in the area. We knew we could expect a sermon that would help us enter even more fully into the spirit of the Christmas season.

Sure enough, the congregational singing, the prayer time, and the special music all invited us to worship. But then something happened that I will not soon forget. The pastor stepped to the pulpit and announced that by the following Sunday the church had to raise over one hundred thousand dollars for its end-of-the-year mortgage payment. Then he went on to make a long appeal for funds.

Though his appeal was as positive and gracious as anyone could have made it, by the time it was finished the spirit of worship had vanished. No longer was our focus on the Christ child; it was on paying the bills.

That morning the pastor went on to preach a sermon every bit as good as I had expected, but I couldn't enjoy it. The long interruption for fund-raising had spoiled the service for me. And since it was the one Sunday of the year when more visitors were there than on any other, no doubt it ruined the morning for many other visitors as well.

Nor did the members welcome the appeal any more than we visitors. This church was so financially strapped that for months the pastor had been asking for funds almost every Sunday. They had long since grown tired of coming to church only to hear yet another request to pay debt.

But of all the people there, the one who most abhorred what happened that morning was the pastor. He had been forced to take on the thankless task of begging people every week to pay a debt far more massive than the church could reasonably bear. He later told me, "The burden of debt is so heavy, sometimes I don't think I'll survive."

Borrowing to Grow

How did this church end up in this predicament? To answer that I have to go back more than twenty years to when they hired me to design their building.

As a church architect I had heard and believed all the usual reasons churches give for building and for borrowing most of the money to do it. And I had become an expert at persuading hesitant church leaders to borrow to build at the earliest opportunity.

When a pastor would wonder if the church could afford the building of their dreams, I knew just what to say. "If we're going to do it, let's do it right. Let's design everything you need." And I'd show him step by step how to qualify for the maximum loan possible.

If a finance committee member objected that the building fund wasn't large enough, I'd say, "Well, of course, you want to raise as much as you can up front, but you can bring in fund-raisers to do that. Remember, the longer you wait, the more it's going to cost. And anyway, with inflation you'll be paying back the loan with cheaper dollars."

Then I'd add the clincher. "Of course, your new building will bring higher attendance, which will generate more giving that will more than cover the interest. Why wait to build when you could be enjoying your building right away while you're paying for it?"

By the time I'd finished my song and dance, almost every church I talked with would be eager to follow my advice. It was, after all, a win-win proposition: They were going to get the building they wanted; I was going to get hired as their architect.

Well, the church Sally and I visited that Christmas had bought wholesale into the borrow-and-build thinking I had so enthusiastically advocated. In the years since the congregation had built, they had continued to borrow for various reasons—each time expecting the project to bring growth. But as I sat in church that Sunday and looked around a sanctuary far from full, even on Christmas Sunday, it was obvious that none of the projects for which the congregation had borrowed had delivered the promised growth.

It's hard to ignore experiences like that, but for many years I managed to convince myself that my borrow-and-build conventional wisdom was basically sound, that church debt problems were exceptions to the rule. They developed only in those few cases where churches foolishly took on excessive debt (something *I* never advocated, of course) or when they ran into unforeseeable problems or when the people refused to give generously enough. So I kept preaching my borrow-and-build philosophy.

A New Direction

I was not one to not practice what I preached. Thirty years into my career I was well along the road to success and was getting pretty good at using "other people's money" to pay for the trip. I was a full partner in an architectural firm with a million dollar payroll and was earning more than I had ever dreamed. Sally could go out and buy anything she wanted, and I didn't have to worry about it. It felt good.

Sally and I lived in a comfortable country home outside Boise, Idaho. We bought ownership in the finest condominium in the resort town of McCall, Idaho. And as an investment and possible future home, we bought one of the best townhouse condominiums in an exclusive development in Boise. In buying each of these homes, we borrowed as much as we could. Next I planned to use one of my three properties as collateral to buy a fourth. And I would have, if God hadn't intervened.

One summer we were visiting our friends James and Shirley Posey in Oklahoma. Just as we were leaving, James handed me a workbook[1] and said, "Ray, you and Sally need to do this Bible study."

I thanked him, took the book home, and set it aside.

Two weeks later James called. "Ray," he asked, "have you and Sally started that Bible study yet?"

"Well, no," I said, grabbing the book off the shelf, "but I have it right here."

James said, "I want you to promise me that you and Sally will start that Bible study today."

So I promised, and that day Sally and I started the book, studying what the Bible has to say about managing money. By the time we finished the workbook later that summer, we were convicted that through the Scripture God was telling us to do two things: simplify our standard of living and get out of debt. Based on those two principles, we set a specific goal—a goal of owning only one house, the one we lived in, and for that house to be paid for, even if that meant moving to a less expensive home.

A few months later one of my partners surprised me with an offer to buy out my share of the architectural firm. I was planning to be an architect the rest of my life, so my first instinct was to turn him down. But as Sally and I prayed about it, we came to believe that God was directing us to accept his offer and leave the firm.

Over the coming months, God revealed bit by bit what was coming next—he was opening the door for us to start a ministry of consulting with churches. Because this would mean a substantial cut in pay, we couldn't have considered it if we hadn't already made big changes in our family finances. We would have had to say, "Sorry, Lord, we can't do the work you're calling us to do. We have to pay our debts." But because we had already said yes to God's direction to live more modestly and get out of debt, we could say yes to God's call.

It was neither easy nor painless, but over the next three years we sold our three homes, moved into another home debt-free, and learned to live comfortably on an income less than half of what we had become accustomed to. We never had to wonder, though, if it was worth it. I had enjoyed my work before, but now Sally and I were able to work together—something we had been wanting to do—and our church consulting work was far more exciting and fulfilling than any work we had ever done before. We saw God using us to help churches and expand their ministries, and we both felt that God had been preparing us our whole lives for this very work.

New Freedom for the Church

We were thrilled with the new freedom to minister we were enjoying because of our simpler, debt-free lifestyle. At first, though, it didn't occur to us that these same principles might benefit churches. I began to consider the possibility only when I noticed how little most of the churches we worked with were able to spend on local outreach.

While all these churches said they were committed to reaching out to their communities, even those with the strongest giving were budgeting little if anything for intentional outreach. Why? What was wrong? I analyzed their budgets, looking for ways to cut expenses to free up money for ministry in the community.

Time after time I was amazed by what a large percentage of their incomes these churches were spending on facilities. Could it be that facility expense, especially interest expense, was a major reason these churches had so little to spend on ministry? What if churches kept building the same buildings, I wondered, but paid for them with cash? What if all the money being spent on interest were redirected to ministry?

Next I realized that many of the churches asking me for construction advice didn't need new buildings at all. Most had better alternatives. Sometimes they needed to remodel or build modest additions, but often they just needed to use the buildings they already had more creatively.

So I started helping churches make better use of their facilities. Some were able to grow to two or even three times the attendance the building had originally been designed for without a new building. These churches were saving not just the cost of interest; they were saving the cost of whole buildings.

Of course, as these churches continued to grow, they did eventually need more space. But because they kept setting aside money for future facility needs, by the time they needed to build, they were long since out of debt and had saved enough to pay most, if not all, of the cost with cash.

By eliminating the construction of entire buildings and by avoiding interest expense when they did build, these churches could save most of the money churches usually pour into buildings—money that could then be used for ministering to people.

The Beg, Borrow, and Steal Syndrome

Once I'd seen churches enjoying this kind of financial freedom, what I'd previously considered normal for church finances no longer looked so normal. I'd been so used to seeing pastors having to beg for money that I'd thought nothing of it. I was so used to churches putting debt payments ahead of spending on ministry that I had accepted it as the way things had to be. And of course, I had not only seen church borrowing as normal; I'd enthusiastically promoted it.

It was eye opening for me to learn that none of these practices were either helpful or necessary. Pastors don't have to beg, congregations don't have to borrow, and churches don't have to "steal" funds from ministry to pay for institutional maintenance. There is a better way.

Part 1 of this book shows how a church can put an end to borrowing. Part 2 spells out how churches can put an end to the inadvertent "stealing" that takes place when funds needed for ministry to people are siphoned off by unnecessarily high expenses for institutional maintenance. Part 3 describes how churches can put an end to begging with a fresh approach to giving that makes raising pledges and special offerings to meet basic operating expenses relics of the past.

As churches strive to avoid or break free of the beg, borrow, and steal syndrome, I believe far more is at stake than how good the church treasurer's report looks. Poor financial decisions can burden, paralyze, or even kill a church, while wise financial decisions can contribute to building up the Christian community and releasing the gifts of its members for life-changing ministry.

If your church is caught up in the beg, borrow, and steal syndrome, even if only slightly, the exciting news is that by applying a few tried and tested principles, your church can enjoy an even greater freedom for ministry, a degree of freedom few churches enjoy.

From Indebtedness to Provision

Selling the Church's Birthright

2

Does church borrowing always lead to problems or is it sometimes a good idea? What dangers does indebtedness pose, and what can churches do to minimize or avoid them? Let's look at the experiences of three actual churches with varying levels of debt.

Case Study #1: Modest Debt

First Church,[1] a congregation of more than two thousand, had a history of strong giving and wise financial management. They had always paid off their mortgages early, then gone on to set aside money each month for their next building program.

As the time for their next building program approached, their architect drafted plans for two major additions. Then in a special offering one Sunday, the church raised over a million dollars for building. With that offering and the money already in the building fund, the church had almost enough to pay for the entire first addition with cash.

With the second addition, though, the church faced a choice. They didn't need the second building right away. The first addition would give them plenty of room to grow. And by waiting three or four years to build the second building, the church could save enough to pay cash for that building as well.

On the other hand, building both additions at once would

avoid the inconvenience of two building programs, and the church could begin using and enjoying the second addition several years sooner than it otherwise could.

The church decided to build both at the same time. Though this meant borrowing about two million dollars, that was a modest debt for this church. It wouldn't endanger any of the church's ministries or require any special fund-raising. The church could simply make the loan payments from the regular weekly offerings.

Case Study #2: Substantial Debt

A few years ago, New Hope Chapel ended the year with a budget surplus and decided to add the entire surplus to their outreach budget. This was possible, the pastor explained, because the church's facility expense was so low. They paid only a modest rent on the little chapel where they worshiped.

This past year that same church, still about seventy-five people, still meeting in the same building, with the level of giving still about the same, faced a different budget picture. Struggling to pay their bills, the church suspended payments for all the outreach ministries they supported. Notices began appearing in the church bulletin telling how far giving had fallen behind budget needs. One notice alerted members that a building payment would soon be due and the church had no money to pay it. Some members began wondering out loud if the church could still afford to pay a full-time pastor.

As the budget year came to a close, giving rallied and the church managed to meet its budget. But what a contrast to the atmosphere of just a few years earlier! Instead of rejoicing in a surplus, the church was laboring just to meet basic expenses. What made the difference?

The main difference was that the church had gone into debt to buy and remodel the chapel where they met. Although they had gotten a bargain price, borrowing just forty thousand dollars to get title to a building valued at seventy thousand dollars, the church's monthly facility expenses had tripled. Because giving had stayed about the same, the higher building expenses forced spending cuts in other areas, and of course, there was no longer any end-of-the-year surplus to be added to the outreach budget.

The dollar amount of New Hope's debt was tiny compared to First Church's two-million-dollar mortgage. But in relation to the congregation's financial strength, New Hope's debt was far heavier. First Church could take its debt in stride. New Hope could pay its debt, but not without a struggle and only by decreasing funding for ministry.

Case Study #3: Heavy Debt

When Pastor Woody Stevens came to Colorado Springs First Church of the Nazarene in 1987, he found a church struggling just to tread water. A year earlier they had completed a major building program—an educational facility and gymnasium—that more than doubled their space. Before the building program, attendance had been declining, and the leaders thought a new building would not only provide more space but get the church growing again.

It hadn't worked. What little growth had taken place had been more than offset when those who didn't want to pay for the new debt left the church. Giving during this same period increased only slightly, not nearly enough to keep pace with the huge jump in building costs. Bottom line: The church was squeezed between huge mortgage payments and less-than-expected giving.

The effects of the financial squeeze were impossible to ignore. The church had absolutely no funds to hire urgently needed staff. Besides that, the original building was overdue for repairs and the new building was of such poor quality that only three years after construction, its roof and flashing were leaking. Though new water stains kept appearing on the walls and ceilings of both buildings, the church couldn't afford to fix the leaks. They just bought buckets to catch the drips.

Both buildings needed painting inside and out, but there was no money to do it. The facilities embarrassed the whole church and frustrated their attempts to attract new people.

Unable to keep up on its loan payments and not even able to pay the fees to refinance its note, the church found itself at the mercy of the bank. In 1990 bank directors began dictating to the church what it had to do to get its finances in order as a condition for refinancing and extending its mortgage.

One Sunday morning the pastor announced in the worship service that the church would be out of toilet paper within the week and that they had no money to buy more. He asked every family to bring a roll of toilet paper with them the next Sunday. I wonder what kind of impression that made on the visitors attending that day.

How did Colorado Springs First Nazarene get into trouble? By subscribing to the same borrow-and-build philosophy I had championed for thirty years. They built far more than they needed, including a gymnasium for which they had no real use, and borrowed almost all the money.

None of this grief was necessary. If, rather than taking on a large debt, the church had met its space needs by using its space more creatively and building a modest addition for which they could have paid most, if not all, of the cost with cash, those long years of financial bondage could have been avoided. Rather than enduring years of struggle, the church could have enjoyed years of financial freedom and a growing ministry.

Less Debt, Greater Freedom

As debt grows heavier, not in dollar amounts but in relation to a church's financial strength, freedom to minister suffers. As debt decreases, the church enjoys a greater financial freedom to minister.

As debt decreases, financial freedom for ministry increases.

This general principle would suggest that the maximum financial freedom for ministry would come when a church is debt-free. Is that true? Let's test that with the church described in the first case study.

First Church made good decisions. They approached their building program in such a way that the church's focus was not shifted to building but remained on ministry. They paid cash for a substantial part of their new construction—about half of it. And they made sure that the new debt would not interfere with existing ministries or slow their growth. The continued growth and financial health of the church since their building program confirm that they made wise decisions.

What might have happened if First Church had chosen the other option—waiting a few years and paying cash for the second building? The interest expense the church would have saved together with the interest income they would have earned on their building fund would have added up to a substantial savings in building costs. How else might First Church have used that money?

Members of First Church were personally involved in a wide range of outreaches in the community—prison ministries, a rescue mission, a shelter and rehabilitation ministry for homeless families, and a food pantry, to name a few. None of these ministries were cut back to make mortgage payments, but I wonder what more could have happened through these and other ministries if the money spent on interest for the second addition had been invested instead in intentional community outreach through ministries like these.

How many more homeless families might the family shelter have been able to take off the streets, training them in life skills and helping them get jobs and get set up in their own homes? How many more people might have gotten involved in recovery groups and found freedom from chemical addiction? What if the church had earmarked, say, fifty thousand dollars a year for community outreach and challenged its members to use that money not only to increase support for existing ministries but also to create new ministries to touch hurting people with God's love? What creativity might have been unleashed?

First Church made a good financial decision, but I believe the option they passed over would have been even better. Their decision

How Debt Affects Freedom to Minister

Level of Debt	Effects on Freedom to Minister
Modest Debt (Debt does not hinder existing ministries.)	• tendency to overlook possibilities to expand existing ministries • tendency to overlook possibilities for creating new ministries • may overlook financial needs of people in the church and community
Substantial Debt (Debt makes it a struggle to maintain effectiveness of existing ministries.)	• some existing ministries operate on less than optimum funding • seriously limits funds available for intentional local outreach • limits funds available for meeting financial needs within the body • makes it almost impossible to launch new ministries
Heavy Debt (Paying debt becomes church's focus, dominating the budget and the time and energy of church leaders.)	• cannot hire needed pastoral or support staff • ministry programs handicapped by underfunding • building maintenance eventually neglected, unloved appearance of building an embarrassment and a barrier to outreach • may cut support staff • may lay off pastoral staff in desperate situations • worst case: foreclosure, bankruptcy, or dissolution of church

to keep their debt modest protected the freedom of their existing ministries; a decision to build debt-free would have given them even more financial freedom, more resources to expand existing ministries and launch new ones.

Years ago when I was working as an architect, I realized excessive borrowing was hurting some churches, so I worked out a formula to help churches borrow safely and avoid taking on too much debt. Some churches are still using this formula. In the years since I developed that formula, though, I've come to realize that the concept of safe borrowing is a lot like safe sex. It's better than nothing because it limits your risks, but it's not the best answer.

Timeless Wisdom

In our credit-driven economy, the suggestion that even modest debt tends to limit freedom may sound like economic heresy. The credit card has become a symbol of freedom. Some companies measure their financial strength in part by how much money financial institutions will lend them. Borrowing and freedom, so the conventional wisdom goes, are two sides of the same coin.

But the Bible describes a different relationship between freedom and debt. Proverbs 22:7 says, "The rich rules over the poor, and the borrower is the slave of the lender." In Israel this slavery was literal. A debtor unable to pay a debt could be forced to work as a slave for a lender for up to seven years. As recently as the early twentieth century, debtors in America who couldn't pay their debts were sentenced to debtors' prison.

The Bible does not say borrowing is a sin,[2] but it does consistently refer to it negatively. In Deuteronomy 15:4–6 God promised the Israelites that if they would obey the commands he was giving them that day, they would lend to many nations and never borrow. He then went on to give them laws to govern their economic life, including instruction to share generously with the poor and needy (vv. 7–12). God did not say it would be a sin for the Israelites to borrow; he said they would need to borrow only if Israel disobeyed God's economic laws.

In Deuteronomy 28:12 a sign of God's blessing on Israel would be that they would lend and not borrow; but if God cursed Israel, one evidence would be that they would borrow and not lend (v. 44). Borrowing was not a privilege but a curse to be avoided.

This principle is just as valid today as it was thirty-five hundred years ago. We are bombarded by ads that urge us to "buy now, pay later," but following that advice often carries a high price tag. Like Esau's selling his birthright for a mess of pottage, when churches borrow they more often than not actually give up something of great long-term value so they can immediately enjoy something of far less value. In exchange for the freedom to build now, when in most cases they don't even need to build, many churches compromise their long-term capacity for ministry.[3]

Some people ask me, "But what if instead of borrowing from a financial institution, we sell bonds to our members? Isn't that okay?" That's better, of course. If you're going to be a slave, it pays to choose your master carefully. But whether your debt payments go to a bank or to church members, the interest—about fifty cents of every dollar paid on debt (depending on the interest rate and the length of the note)—is money that cannot go to ministry.

Bad financial decisions in the past or special circumstances may make some church borrowing necessary or advisable, and the next chapter will consider these exceptions. But as a general rule, avoiding debt whenever possible is still the safest guide, both for individual Christians and for the church. This is the path that leads both individual Christians and the body of Christ to the greatest possible financial freedom for doing God's work in the world.

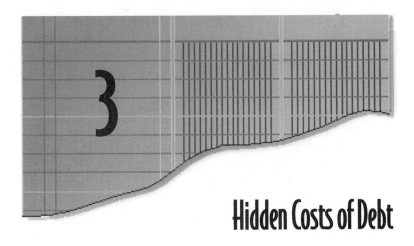

Hidden Costs of Debt

When I first started designing church buildings, many of the churches I worked for would take out loans based on my cost estimates only to run out of money before the job was finished. They would then have to go back to the bank for a second loan. Were my estimates really that far off?

No. The problem was that I would prepare estimates only for those parts of the project I had been hired to design. The churches, when calculating how much they needed to borrow, would often simply forget to figure in other standard costs. They would forget to budget for such expenses as professional fees for architects, engineers, and attorneys; permits; assessments; surveys; platting; interest on the construction loan; hooking up utilities; landscaping; furniture and equipment; moving expenses; and more. So churches wouldn't keep making this mistake, I started creating a budget for the entire project, not just for those parts I had been hired to design.

When it comes to calculating the cost of borrowing, many churches make the same mistake. When I ask a church how much they owe on their loan, without exception they tell me the principal balance. The interest is not included, even though the church owes the interest just as surely as they owe the principal. Even more often overlooked, however, is the impact church borrowing can have on the church's ministries and on the spiritual lives of members. There is no reason these "hidden costs" need to come as any more of a surprise than the cost of church furnishings. When they are hidden it is because we have become blind to them as a result of being immersed in a credit economy where borrowing is considered normal, healthy, even necessary; where borrowing's benefits are exaggerated and its costs often overlooked.

As we have already seen, the Bible does not share this naively optimistic view of debt. Scripture can remove our cultural blinders revealing these hidden costs of debt. Then we can approach the decision to borrow or not to borrow with our eyes wide open to the actual costs.

Four Consequences of Church Debt

Consequence #1: *By presuming on the future, borrowing puts the church at unnecessary risk.* James writes, "Come now, you who say, 'Today or tomorrow we will go to such and such a town and spend a year there, doing business and making money.' Yet you do not even know what tomorrow will bring. . . . As it is, you boast in your arrogance; all such boasting is evil" (James 4:13–16).

Most borrowing is based on presumptuous financial predictions. I used to tell churches that a new building would lead to higher attendance and more giving and advised them to apply for a loan based on these optimistic projections. It was bad advice, and following it has brought grief to many churches. Buildings don't make churches grow, and as James points out, we don't know what our income will be next year.

Though it is less risky than assuming an increase, it is still presumptuous to borrow on the assumption that the church's income will remain the same. Most churches go through periods of declining income. When a local military base or major industry closes, not only can the church's income decrease, but some who previously contributed generously may have financial needs that the church will need to be prepared to meet.

Church income can also drop when a group of people leaves the church. When is this most likely to happen? When the church is struggling financially. Pastors often tell me, "The very people who voted to get us into debt are the ones who left when things got tough."

Ironically, borrowing against projected growth can actually hinder growth. Why? Because debt often increases financial stress and makes less money available for the ministries that can lead to growth.

In contrast, operating debt-free prepares the church to not only weather an economic downturn but to financially assist both members and nonmembers during economic hard times. At the same time, it poises the church to take full advantage of times of abundance to use increased income to expand ministries rather than to pay debt.

Consequence #2: *Borrowing tends to undermine contentment.* Paul wrote the Philippians that he had learned to be content with whatever he had, whether it was little or much (Phil. 4:12–13). He wrote Timothy that "there is great gain in godliness combined with contentment" (1 Tim. 6:6). Hebrews 13:5 exhorts us, "Keep your lives free from the love of money, and be content with what you have." In a culture where greed is considered normal, sometimes even virtuous, the biblical message of contentment is urgently needed.

The main reason people borrow is because they are not content to live within their income. The church is responsible to teach its members to reject the always-wanting-more mentality of the world and to choose to be content with God's provision. The most powerful way the church can teach contentment with God's provision is by example. If the church preaches contentment but does not live it, its actions will undermine its words.

Pastor Randy Alcorn, whose church (Good Shepherd Community Church in Gresham, Oregon) has committed to never borrow money, writes, "If we are to encourage our people to live as much as possible without going into debt, it seems only reasonable that we would operate that way as a church. What is right for church families is right for the church family."[1]

Consequence #3: *Borrowing can deprive us of God's timing.* John 14:14 says, "If in my name you ask me for anything, I will do it." If God has directed us to pursue a particular ministry or project, we can confidently ask him to supply the resources to make it possible.

When God provides the money for such a project, we gratefully take God's provision as confirmation of his guidance to move ahead. But are we just as willing to accept God's withholding of funds as guidance—as instruction to wait or even as a closed door?

Faith acts in obedience to guidance from God. Presumption, on the other hand, decides what to do and when, then asks God to bless it. Borrowing can be a way of getting around God's no, a way to move ahead on our own timetable rather than waiting for God's.

Consequence #4: *Borrowing can blind us to people's needs.* When Paula (not her real name) was almost killed by an electrical shock in her home, the family immediately replaced the defective electrical panel responsible for the accident. Because they didn't have the seven hundred dollars needed for the repair, a member of their small group suggested that church families pitch in to pay for it. He felt that sharing within the body of Christ should insure that no financial need within the body goes unmet (Acts 4:34). In the discussion that followed, someone said, "But lots of people make payments on things."

This church did end up generously helping the family, but in many similar situations churches have done nothing. When churches operate out of a debt-is-normal mindset, they can be blinded to the legitimate needs of their members caused by health emergencies, unemployment, family crises, or accidents. Because they don't recognize the financial need and the responsibility of the body of Christ to respond to it, they force their members into the slavery of indebtedness.

When the church as a whole is committed to living within God's provision, emergencies that threaten to create involuntary indebtedness for church members are seen for what they are—opportunities for the church to demonstrate caring and to protect fellow members' financial freedom through generous sharing.

Business Debt versus Church Debt

In addition to these biblical reasons for avoiding debt, I've come to realize that for the church, going into debt is usually bad business. Debt does have some practical advantages for profit-making businesses, but none of them apply to the church.

What advantages do businesses receive from buying property with debt?

1. *Business property produces income.* Business owners borrow to buy real estate because they expect the property to generate more than enough income to make the mortgage payments. They expect the property to generate a profit.

   Church buildings don't produce income. Churches do not receive business income from their buildings. For churches, the cost of buildings is an expense, not a business investment.

2. *Business property usually appreciates.* Business owners may prefer to buy buildings, even with heavy indebtedness, rather than rent, because good quality buildings usually increase in value.

   But the resale value of church buildings decreases rapidly. Generally a church building's market value is fifty cents on the dollar, or less, compared to the book value. This means a church facility that costs one million dollars to build will usually have a resale value of a half million dollars or less the moment it is finished.

3. *Business debt brings tax advantages.* Interest on business debt is tax deductible. Businesses can deduct depreciation expense on buildings, even when their market value is appreciating. Depending on the tax laws in effect at the time, profits from the sale of business property (capital gains) may be taxed at a lower rate than other business income. All operating expenses related to business buildings—such as utilities, insurance, repairs, and custodial services—are tax deductible.

   Churches get no tax advantages from owning property, because they don't pay income taxes.

4. *Businesses can use real estate as leverage to make further investments.* Once real estate investors build up equity in property, they can borrow against that equity to buy more property.

   Church property cannot be leveraged.

5. *If a business gets into financial trouble, it can declare bankruptcy.* Most business debt involves risk, so it's a normal part of doing business for some investments to go sour, sometimes leading to

bankruptcy. Corporations can go bankrupt, yet the owners' personal finances are not at risk. The owners can use the bankruptcy laws to avoid personal responsibility, then go on with their lives.

A church cannot declare bankruptcy without dissolving the church. Besides the fact that bankruptcy ends a church's existence, God's people have a moral responsibility to repay all legitimate debts, no matter how difficult repayment may be. It is the "wicked" who "borrow and do not pay back" (Ps. 37:21).

So while debt has both benefits and risks for the business owner, the church that borrows assumes all the risks of debt without enjoying any of these benefits.

For all these reasons I no longer promote the conventional wisdom of borrow and build but advocate what I call the principle of provision: *A church should build only when it can do so within the income God has provided and without using funds needed for the church's present and future ministries.*

For the last fifteen years I have recommended this principle to the growing churches I have worked with. The results I have witnessed in those churches that have embraced this approach have more than confirmed to me that provision, not indebtedness, is the road to the church's greatest possible financial freedom for ministry.

A Time to Borrow?

In light of all these disadvantages of debt, is there ever a time to borrow? I believe there is. While a church enjoys the greatest possible financial freedom for ministry when it operates debt-free, seldom can this goal be achieved overnight. In several situations I have advised churches to take on temporary debt as part of an overall plan to become debt-free in the long run.

Situation #1: *It may be better to borrow when renting would cost more.* Sometimes reasonably priced rental space is not available. When the cost of buying—including mortgage payments, insurance, maintenance, repairs, utilities, etc.—is less than the cost of renting, buying may be the better option.

Buying and renting, however, may not be the only alternatives. When the rent of a small congregation in the Los Angeles area suddenly shot up, the church had no choice but to find less expensive meeting space. Its solution was to become a cell-based church. The congregation formed into several cells—small groups that meet in homes—and made the cell meetings the primary meetings of the church. Gatherings of the entire congregation took place less often, sharply decreasing the church's need for large-group meeting space.[2]

If renting is prohibitive, don't assume that you have to borrow. Explore a variety of creative ways to meet your church's space needs.

Situation #2: *Sometimes it pays to borrow to buy income-generating property to provide space for future growth.* I do not recommend the church's buying rental property to generate income, but sometimes it is a good idea for a church to buy property for future expansion. If a residence next to the church campus comes on the market and the church expects to need that property within the next few years, the church may want to consider buying it, even if it involves carrying a mortgage.

Borrowing to buy such a property is wise only if the purchase meets the following conditions.

- *Rent income covers most or all expenses,* including mortgage payments, maintenance, insurance, and all other operating expenses.
- *The house stands alone as collateral for the note.* Most mortgages stipulate that if a borrower cannot meet the payments, the lender can sell the house and apply the proceeds against the note. If the sale doesn't bring enough to cover the note, the borrower still owes the balance. Such contracts run the risk of "true debt"—a loan that the borrower lacks the resources to repay.

  To avoid this risk, take out a mortgage only if the mortgage includes an exculpatory clause stating that the house stands as full collateral for the note. This way all the church risks is what it has invested in the house; the church's ongoing ministries are not at risk.

- *The resale value of the house exceeds the loan amount.* If the church cannot make the payments, it can sell the house and pay off the note.

- *The note can be paid off by the time the church needs to use the property.* If the church expects to start using the property in five years, take out a five-year note. Then the church will own the property debt-free by the time it needs to convert it from rental to church use.

- *No money is taken from ministry to pay for the property.* Where will the church get the money for the down payment and a reserve fund to cover periods of vacancy, emergency repairs, and other costs above regular monthly expenses? The church should not buy the property unless it can meet these needs without taking money from its ministries.

- *People other than pastoral staff are able and willing to manage the rental property.* Managing rental property can be a time-consuming job involving lots of hassles. Pastoral staff should never have to take time from pastoring to manage church-owned rental property.

When the church buys and manages a rental property by these guidelines, no funds are diverted from the ministries of the church, and the rental income becomes a form of provision for future expansion.

Situation #3: *Churches often must borrow during their transition from a debt economy to a provision economy.* Once a church commits to becoming and staying debt-free, it may take ten years or longer for it to pay off its debt and save enough so that future buildings can be paid for with cash. If construction is needed during that transition period, it may require some borrowing. To refuse to borrow during this period could cripple the church's ministry by forcing the church to do without desperately needed staff or facilities.

Such borrowing should be viewed as a temporary necessity resulting from the church's previous practice of operating on a debt economy. As the church consistently makes decisions to avoid debt when practical and hold it to a minimum when it is truly needed, the church will experience growing financial freedom and can eventually be free of debt.

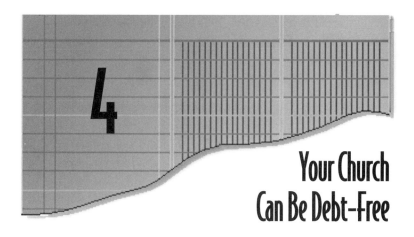

Your Church Can Be Debt-Free

Your church can get out of debt and stay out of debt, but it won't be easy. Making the transition from a debt economy to a cash economy takes courage, tenacity, and resolve. It takes spiritually rooted motivation. And it takes a plan.

In 1981 Fairview Village Church in the Philadelphia area asked me to design a thousand-seat sanctuary for them. When I got there, I saw at once why the church wanted more space. As I entered the foyer, I had to step over school children lying on pallets. Walking down the hallway I had to thread my way through school furniture and equipment and more sleeping children.

The next Sunday morning the sanctuary was packed, even with the children worshiping separately. Sunday school classes were crammed into every available space. Yes, this church had an urgent space problem.

But they also had a debt problem. The church had made good choices about the kinds of facilities they had built, and they had paid reasonable prices. But as most churches do, they had borrowed most of the money to pay for its buildings. The church still owed on their last building and almost all the money for any new building would have to be borrowed.

I had come to Fairview Village expecting to design a sanctuary. But as I analyzed the church's finances, I reached a surprising conclusion: Rather than enabling the church to keep growing, a major building program at that time would probably kill the church's growth. They simply didn't have the funds to build without taking money away from present and future ministries. A major building program at that time could not help but change the church's focus from people to buildings.

So instead of drawing up plans for a thousand-seat sanctuary, I drew up a plan for Fairview Village's transition from a debt economy to a provision economy. Yet even before I presented the plan to the church growth committee, I knew that for the plan to have a chance of succeeding, the church would have to meet two prerequisites.

Prerequisite #1: Put People First

A church that looks at the size or appearance of its building as a measure of the church's success is unlikely to make the transition to provision; it probably won't be interested in the smaller-scale multi-purpose kind of building needed for a church to be able to make the transition to a cash economy.

A church that sees building buildings as the work of the church will want to keep building buildings as fast as it can; it won't want to wait until it can pay cash to build.

Few growing churches can get out of debt and stay out of debt unless they first change how they use, design, and pay for buildings. And for a congregation to be willing to make such significant changes, they must see buildings not as ends in themselves, not as signs of success or importance, but as tools pure and simple.

Church leaders must be absolutely clear that the purpose of the church is not to build an institution but to minister to people's needs. Any church where people truly come first will welcome any strategy that enables it put less time, money, and energy into buildings, and more time, money, and energy into ministering to people.

From the day I first arrived at Fairview Village, it was clear to me that in that church people came first. The church was growing rapidly almost entirely through evangelizing unchurched people.

They weren't interested in coming up with reasons to justify a building program; they simply wanted enough space to accommodate their growing ministry to people. They had already met the first prerequisite.

Prerequisite #2: Count the Cost

Before a church can make the transition from a debt economy to a provision economy, the people must first count the cost and commit to paying it. They have to understand that the transition will be extremely difficult. They must realize that it will take time, probably many years. They will probably have to significantly increase their giving. No church should set out on this course unless the people of the church are determined to follow through, whatever the price. Without such resolve, no church will reach this goal.

For the plan to succeed at Fairview Village, the people would have to be motivated by a deep-seated spiritual commitment to adopt it. If they agreed to it for any lesser reasons, they wouldn't be prepared to make the necessary sacrifices in giving, they wouldn't have the resolve to stick with the plan year after year when the old way of doing things looked easier. But if their hearts were fully in it, they could do it. They could throw off the burden of debt.

The people of the church would also have to truly believe that God knew their needs even better than they did, and that they could trust him to fully provide for those needs. By choosing to be content with what God had provided, the people would no longer feel the need to borrow, to live beyond the church's means.

Such trust is a spiritual matter, and the commitment to live within what God provided would have to be a spiritual commitment. Were the people of Fairview Village prepared to make this commitment? I would soon find out. I was ready to present the plan.

The master plan I prepared for Fairview Village consisted of two parts—a facility plan and a financial plan. While each church must develop facility and financial plans tailored to its own needs, these same basic steps will work for most growing churches.

The Facility Plan

Step 1: *Fully utilize present facilities.* Most churches that think they need to build aren't fully using the space they already have. While some changes in use cost money, many require nothing more than a new way of thinking about facilities and a willingness to do things differently, including a willingness to be inconvenienced for the work of the church.

I recommended that Fairview Village make the following changes immediately.

- *Move classes to the right size rooms.* Some Sunday school classes were crowded while others had room to spare. Moving large classes to large rooms and small classes to small rooms would give larger classes room to keep growing.
- *Cap school enrollment.* The church's Christian school was over-running the building. Capping enrollment would enable the school to move back into appropriate boundaries so the church could use the building for other activities during the week.
- *Build a storage shed.* Fairview Village was using three rooms for storage. One was carpeted and had windows and heat and air conditioning—none of which were needed for storage. A low-cost storage shed would free up these three rooms for use by the Sunday school and Christian school.
- *Replace pews with chairs.* Good church chairs are not cheap, but they cost far less than a new building. By replacing pews with chairs, Fairview Village could make its largest single space, the worship area, useful for ministry seven days a week.

Step 2: *Remodel for multiple use.* Minor remodeling can make a major difference in a space's usefulness. Churches can often increase usable space by taking a wall out or putting one in, or by installing a folding wall across part of a foyer or hallway.

On its property Fairview Village had a historic barn with little usable space. Remodeling could transform it into a gymnasium, kitchen, and educational space at half the cost of new construction.

Step 3: *Build an addition that increases the usefulness of present facilities.* Most rooms in traditional church buildings are designed for just one use—the sanctuary for worship, classrooms for classes, the gymnasium for recreation. For a steadily growing church to get out of debt and stay out of debt, it has to make multiple use of most or all of its space. Sometimes all it takes to convert to multiple use of space is deciding to do it. Sometimes it requires changing furnishings, such as buying adjustable-height tables. And sometimes it may call for substantial remodeling or additions.

Most rapidly growing churches must hold multiple worship services so the size of their facilities does not limit their growth. To accommodate multiple services, a church needs a fellowship foyer big enough that those leaving one service have room to visit with those arriving for the next. Fairview Village needed to go to double services but had only a small foyer designed for a single service.

I suggested the church build a new fellowship foyer, including urgently needed office space in the addition. At the same time they could remove the wall between the old foyer and worship space. This would expand worship seating from 250 to 300, giving the church room to grow to 600 with double services.

Step 4: *Build a new building.* After the first three steps of the facility plan, Fairview Village would be fully utilizing its present facility, so the next step would be to build. Their next building would not, though, be the thousand-seat sanctuary I had been asked to design. The church's worship space needs could be met far more easily by adding a third service.

But by then the church would need more educational space. So I recommended a two-story building with classrooms for Sunday school and the elementary school on the first level and a large multipurpose room with a soundproof movable wall system on the second floor.

If the church continued to grow, it would eventually need to build a thousand-seat ministry center.

The Financial Plan

The second part of Fairview Village's master plan was the financial plan. By fully using their space in each phase of the facility plan, the church could spend far less than expected on facilities. That made it possible to develop a financial plan that met facility needs without taking funds away from present or future ministries.

Step 1: *Start with the least expensive changes in use of space.* While parts of the facility plan would cost a lot, some changes cost little or nothing. The changes listed in step 1 of the facility plan could all be implemented within months.

Step 2: *Ask the congregation to increase giving to get the church out of debt as quickly as possible without sacrificing spending on staff and ministry.*

Step 3: *Once the debt is paid, set aside money monthly with the goal of paying cash for at least half of the next major building project.* In Fairview Village's case, this would be the fellowship foyer and worship space remodeling (step 3 of the facility plan). Since the fellowship foyer was overdue, the church couldn't postpone building it until they could pay cash for the entire project. Seldom can a church move from a debt economy to a cash economy in a single step.

Step 4: *Continue to set aside the same percentage of income for building.* By setting aside a percentage of income rather than a dollar amount, the amount set aside each month would increase as the church grew and giving increased. This fund would first retire the debt from the new building, then begin accumulating toward the next building project.

Step 5: *Pay cash to build the next building, completing the transition to a cash economy.*

The Church's Response

That was the plan I presented. The people committed themselves to it wholeheartedly and went to work. In less than a year they had paid off the mortgage. In about two years they were able to add the fellowship foyer, paying cash for more than half of it. Attendance and giving kept increasing. Within two years after completing the addition, the church was once again debt-free.

The church grew faster than expected with average attendance reaching 850 by 1989, so a third service was added and the next building—the two-story educational facility—was built sooner than planned. Of the $1.2 million construction cost, $850,000 was on hand when construction began, and the rest was raised during construction. The church completed the building with no debt. Just eight years after the church committed itself to living within its income, it had completed the transition from indebtedness to provision.

How much did Fairview Village save by implementing this plan? First, by changing facility usage from single use to intensive multiple use, the church reduced by 40 percent the amount of floor space needed for each person. That alone reduced facility costs by 40 percent.

Second, by eliminating interest expense and instead earning interest income, the church reduced the cost of construction, as compared to a conventional twenty-year note at the prevailing interest rate, by 60 percent of the remaining cost, for a total savings of 75 percent compared to traditional single-use construction and debt financing.

Most important, by adopting this strategy rather than building a huge sanctuary that could have crushed them financially, the church kept its focus on people rather than having it diverted to building. During these eight years, the church launched creative new ministries, and the church's growth continued uninterrupted through all phases of the plan.

Can It Happen in Your Church?

There was nothing unique about Fairview Village's situation that made it particularly easy to make the transition to a provision economy. What made the difference was the people's passion for ministry and their willingness to wholeheartedly support a strategy that kept them focused on people rather than buildings. If the people of your church share that passion and are willing to back it up with a similar commitment, yes, it can happen in your church too.

Understanding how debt is paid and how much it costs can help you make a wiser decision when considering borrowing to build. If your church is already paying debt, fill out all five items. If you are con-

1. Costs Up Front

List all the costs of initiating the loan:

Points for making the loan $_____

Credit analysis $_____

Paperwork/preparation $_____

Appraisal $_____

Mortgage preparation $_____

Filing $_____

Other costs $_____

Total costs $_____

2. True Debt

Principal amount borrowed $_____

For number of years

_____

At percent interest

_____%*

Total interest

Monthly payment amount

$_____

Times number of months

x_____

Minus principal amount

-$_____

Equals total interest $_____

**True debt:
principal + interest** $_____

* If the interest rate is variable, estimate an average for this study.

sidering borrowing, fill out items one through four to determine what the loan would actually cost. You may need to ask your lender for some of these numbers.

It takes the same dollars to pay interest as to pay the principal. Most churches cannot be sure debt will be paid ahead of schedule. Show true debt when showing the amount in your financial statements.

3. Time Is Money

The longer you take to repay the debt, the more the interest. Example: You borrow $1000 at a 9% interest rate.

Years	Monthly Payment	Total Paid	Interest Paid
30	$8.05	$2898	$1898
15	$10.15	$1829	$827

Savings in years: 15 years   Savings in interest: $1071

Cost of savings: just $2.10 increase in monthly payment

If you decide to borrow, at least minimize your "loss."

Insert your proposed or existing loan numbers, using a comprehensive mortgage payment tables book to find the numbers.

Years	Monthly Payment	Total Paid	Interest Paid
_____	$_____	$_____	$_____
_____	$_____	$_____	$_____

Savings in years: _____   Savings in interest: $_____

Cost of savings: $_____ increase in monthly payment

4. When You Pay Interest

You pay most interest up front and most of the principal at the end of the payments.

Example: $100,000 borrowed for 15 years at 12% interest, monthly payment $1,200.

	Interest Paid	Principal Paid
First 5 years	$55,700	$16,300
Last 5 years	$18,000	$54,000

The lender does not make much during the last part of repayment. This is why many notes will not let you pay extra on the principal during the early years of the loan.

Insert your existing or proposed loan numbers in the example. Use the comprehensive mortgage payment tables for numbers.

	Interest Paid	Principal Paid
First 5 years	$_____	$_____
Last 5 years	$_____	$_____

5. The Price of Freedom

Do this analysis of your current debt.

Amount borrowed (original principal) $ _____

Years: ___ Interest: ___ % Payment: $ _____

How much paid to date on principal? $ _____

Principal balance remaining to be paid $ _____

How much interest paid to date? $ _____

Interest remaining to be paid
on present payment schedule $ _____

Remaining principal + remaining interest=
True debt balance to be paid $ _____

Even a small amount added to each payment will save time and money. If you are near the end of your repayment schedule, however, your interest savings may be small. In that case if those funds are needed for other growth or ministry needs, it is often better to follow the regular payment schedule.

From Institutionalism to Purpose

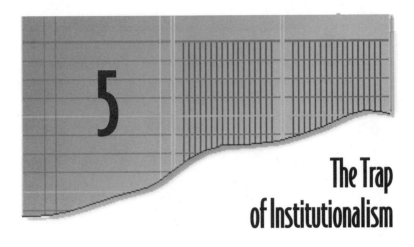

5

The Trap
of Institutionalism

I heard the other day of an organization started to relieve a certain special evil," writes missiologist Roland Allen. "It was reported that means might be found to wipe out this evil. The first expression of the directors was not one of joy at such a glorious prospect, but of anxiety for their organization. If this happens, they said, what will become of our organization? And they were quite relieved when they were assured that there would be plenty of work for them to do for many years to come."[1]

We smile at this incident, but we also find it altogether believable, even to be expected. It is a graphic example of institutionalism, which Allen describes as "a horrible tendency for an organization to grow in importance till it overshadows the end of its existence, and begins to exist for itself."[2]

We've all come across organizations created for some worthy cause that have since become preoccupied with their own institutional growth or survival. Such an organization no longer measures its success primarily by whether it is accomplishing its mission; it defines success in institutional terms. So for example, a charitable organization created to fight poverty may boast of a good year because contributions are up and they have expanded staff and built a new facility, even if no families have escaped poverty through the charity's work that year.

The Mission of the Church

"The church as the body of Christ does not exist for itself," write Richards and Hoeldtke. "The body of Christ exists to carry out the continuing mission of Jesus."[3] And what is the mission of Jesus? It includes bringing glory to God, reconciling people to God and one another, healing broken bodies and spirits, caring for the poor and oppressed, working for justice, and much more.

But the church, like any other organization, can be seduced by institutionalism. It can be lulled into thinking that whenever the church can point to increases in the three Bs—bucks, bodies, and buildings[4]—it must be advancing God's kingdom. Many churches get caught up in pouring most of their time, money, and energy into maintaining the church's structures and programs, and the church's mission gets little more than lip service.

A Christian church in the Northwest adopted one of the strongest mission statements I have ever read. Among many other good things, it said, "We are committed to helping people discover, refine, and use their spiritual gifts." "To reach as many people as possible . . . we commit ourselves to a multiple offense in evangelism." "We are committed to helping people confront their workplaces, schools, places of leisure, and communities with Christian principles." "We believe people experience spiritual growth when they are entrusted with specific ministry tasks and given the responsibility to accomplish them." "We are committed to a stewardship focus that emphasizes others, not selfish interests."

Not only did the church's mission statement sound these themes, they were carried through in the church's one-year goals.

When I arrived at the church to begin my work I asked the pastor, "What are you doing to carry out these wonderful statements?"

While a few individuals were reaching out, the pastor could point to almost nothing the church as a whole was doing to carry out its good intentions. Though this church claimed to be committed to equipping people for evangelism, they were offering no evangelism training. They said they wanted to help people identify, develop, and use their spiritual gifts, but they offered no regular teaching on spiritual gifts and had no specific way to help people identify or test their gifts.

Among the most telling signs was their spending. While the church said they wanted their stewardship to emphasize others, not selfish interests, they were spending 87 percent of their budget on institutional maintenance (facilities, staff, and operations) and only 13 percent on ministry to others. Only 2 1/2 percent was going toward meeting the needs of people in the community. This church was not putting its money where its mission statement was.

When I met with the church's lay leaders one Saturday and pointed out that they were not implementing major parts of their mission statement, they were shocked. "You don't need to rewrite your mission statement," I told them. "You just need to start doing it."

The Church Off Course

How we spend our money, whether as individuals or churches, reveals more about our priorities than what we say. Suppose I claim to care deeply about the poor. At the same time, I say that while I enjoy playing golf, it's not particularly important to me; I can take it or leave it. Yet when you look at my check ledger, you see that I spend more on golf than I do on helping people in financial need. You will probably suspect that contrary to what I say, playing golf is in fact more important to me than ministering to the poor.

The same test applies to the church. If a church says, for example, that it is deeply committed to reaching out to hurting people in its community, but it budgets only 2 percent of its income for that purpose, which will you believe—its words or its actions?

A church's budget is a prime indicator of its true priorities. When it doesn't put its money where its mission statement is, the church is off course. Like an airplane whose flight plan does not match its stated destination, it cannot reach its intended destination unless it changes direction.

Diagnosing Imbalance

How can your church budget help you gauge your present priorities and identify where changes in emphasis may be needed? It's not quite as easy as it might sound. When I first look at a church's budget, seldom can I tell how much it spends on facilities, staff, operations, or sharing. Spending for each of these items is often scattered throughout several budget categories.

But it is possible to translate your budget into a form that allows you to measure how well your budget priorities line up with your declared mission. You can then identify any imbalances, set goals, and monitor your progress toward the goals you have set. Here is one way to do this.

Step 1: *Divide your spending into six categories.* Go through your budget, line by line, assigning each dollar of spending to one of the following categories. Three of these categories—facilities, staff, and operations—pay for the maintenance of church structures and for ministry programs serving both those within and outside the church. The other three categories are for sharing—money the church gives to meet the needs of people outside the community, people in the community, and people within the church.

Maintenance and Ministries	Sharing
Facilities	People outside the Community
Staff	People in the Community
Operations	People within the Church

Here is what I include in each categtory.

Facilities. This includes three subcategories: (1) debt payments (or rent), (2) capital improvements (including savings for future capital improvements), and (3) building expenses. Building expenses include interest, maintenance and repairs, insurance, utilities, lawn care, and custodial services.

Staff. This includes the salaries, benefits, and expenses for all professional and support staff.

Operations. This has two subcategories: (1) church operations and (2) office operations.

Church operations includes money spent on all the programs and activities of the church, such as Sunday school, worship services, youth activities, children's programs, recreation programs, church socials, and programs of outreach.

Office operations includes all nonstaff spending for running the church office.

Sharing with people outside the community. I define a church's local community as that radius within which 90 percent of the members live. If 90 percent of your members live within a ten-mile radius of the church's meeting place, missions giving to people outside your community would include all giving that goes to ministries more than ten miles from your facility. Most giving to mission organizations falls in this category.

Sharing with people in your community. This category includes any financial assistance your church provides to people not a part of your church who live within the area where 90 percent of your members live. It also includes funds that the church gives to other local ministries in which your church is a partner, particularly those in which church members personally minister, such as a food pantry, shelter, or clinic.

Sharing with people within your church. This category includes all financial assistance your church provides for people who attend your church. This can take the form of emergency financial assistance during a time of illness, unemployment, or trauma. It could include helping a family with education or transportation expenses so the family can avoid going into debt. It might involve providing regular monthly support for a family so a single mother can be at home nurturing her children rather than leaving them in day care all day.

Maintenance and Ministries	Sharing

Facilities
  debt payments
  capital improvements
  building expenses
	People outside the Community
	  people outside radius
	  missions

Staff
  salaries
  benefits
  expenses
	People in the Community
	  nonmembers inside radius
	  other local ministries

Operations
  church operations
  office operations
	People within the Church
	  emergency financial assistance
	  assistance to avoid debt
	  monthly support

Once you have divided your expenses into these six categories, total the amounts and calculate what percentage of your budget is going to each of the six categories.

Step 2: *Compare maintenance and ministry spending to sharing.* Add the amounts your church spends on facilities, staff, and operations to get the total spent on maintenance and ministry. Then add the amounts spent on the three sharing categories. How does the percentage your church spends on keeping the church running compare with the percentage you give to others?

This ratio can indicate whether the church has fallen victim to institutionalism—operating primarily to maintain its own existence. It's not that spending on the maintenance of the church is bad; in fact, it's absolutely necessary. The thing to watch for is balance. When a church spends a lot on itself while giving comparatively little to others, it may reveal a consumer mentality. Do the members view the church mainly in terms of what it can do for them rather than in terms of how they can serve others?

Step 3: *Compare your three sharing categories.* Does your budget reflect a balance? Giving to world missions is important, but it is no substitute for personal involvement in ministry to people in need right on our doorstep. For every dollar a church spends on missions for people outside the community, I recommend that it also spend a dollar for sharing with people within the community, preferably supporting ministries in which church members can and will personally participate.

Of the six budget categories, there is one I seldom find in church budgets—sharing with people within the church. Some churches spontaneously respond to emergency needs of people within the church, and that is good, but the absence of a budget line shows the church is not prepared to consistently meet these needs.

This is all the more striking when we realize that in the New Testament, this was probably the church's highest financial priority. Acts 4:34–35 says, "There was not a needy person among them, for as many as owned lands or houses sold them and brought the proceeds of what was sold. They laid it at the apostles' feet, and it was distributed to each as any had need." These early Christians shared so consistently and so generously with one another that every financial need within the body of Christ was cared for. What a witness that must have been to a watching world! How much of the Jerusalem church's phenomenal growth took place because people were in awe of a love so powerful that it would not let any financial need within the church community go unmet?

Paul exhorted the Galatians to "do good to all people, especially to those who belong to the family of believers" (Gal. 6:10 NIV). While we are to share with all people in need, the needs of our brothers and sisters in Christ come first. If legitimate financial needs within a local church fellowship are being neglected, those unmet needs reveal the church's lack of love: "How does God's love abide in anyone who has the world's goods and sees a brother or sister in need and yet refuses help?" (1 John 3:17).

The Church's Highest Financial Priority

While meeting needs within the body is the most neglected category of spending in many churches, I believe Scripture calls us to make it our first priority. This will not necessarily mean we will spend more on this category than on any other; it will mean, though, that we adopt "no unmet financial need within the local body of believers" as our minimum standard. For the obedient church, demonstrating our love and care for one another in this way will take priority over all other spending.

I have worked with churches whose leaders assumed their people did not have such needs or had them only rarely. In reality every church has needs of this kind, but in our individualistic society we have forgotten how to recognize them.

Financial needs are not confined to the poor. Even in the most affluent congregations people lose their jobs. They experience emergencies not fully covered by insurance. When affluent families go through divorce, unemployment, major illness, or bereavement, they often need counseling. The same traumas that create the need for counseling often leave families unable to pay for it. These are usually not the kinds of needs the church can raise funds for publicly; the funds must be designated in advance.

These needs can be met in various ways, and which way is most appropriate depends on the circumstances. Many needs, both within and outside the church, can best be met through a "Sharing Fund" line item in the budget. This demonstrates that the church considers meeting such needs to be an essential part of its mission, not something it does only on special occasions.

In churches that have small groups, when a need arises within a group, the other families can chip in to share the burden. This can be a wonderful way of tangibly showing love and strengthening community.

Sometimes it is best for one person or family to give directly to another person or family. In other cases a public appeal may help to unify the church behind a family going through a difficult time.

Sometimes there are specific reasons that make it most appropriate to give anonymously. At other times community is strengthened when the receiver knows who the givers are.

As a general rule, a "Sharing Fund" check should not be mailed. Rarely does a church have a better opportunity to minister to someone who is hurting, either within the church or outside it, than when a representative of the church is delivering the check. Remember, the check is only a vehicle; the primary goal is communicating love and strengthening the relationship.

However we go about it, we can develop a sensitivity to these needs and learn to respond to them in ways that make the recipients feel honored and cared for rather than demeaned and embarrassed, and in ways that will make a powerful witness. But it will not happen unless we are intentional about it. A good place to start is to affirm that such sharing within the body of Christ is to be the church's highest financial priority.

Breaking Free

Every church is vulnerable to the trap of institutionalism—putting the maintenance of institutional structures ahead of the church's mission. When the church becomes a self-serving institution, it makes it more difficult for its members to fulfill their callings in the world rather than empowering them to do so, and the church's witness is seriously compromised. As Howard Snyder writes, "It is hard to escape the conclusion that today one of the greatest roadblocks to the gospel of Jesus Christ is the institutional church."[5]

But it is possible for a church to move from institutionalism to purpose, to refocus time, money, and energy on the mission that originally called it into being. The next chapter will explore how a church can free its pastoral staff from preoccupation with chores of institutional maintenance so they can invest their best energy in the real mission of the church. Then chapter 7 will look at how reprioritizing spending can help a church break out of a maintenance mindset and renew its vision for putting the needs of people ahead of the demands of the institution.

Freeing Spiritual Leaders to Lead

If your church were looking for a pastor, what kind of response do you think you would get if you ran an ad something like this?

WANTED: Pastor to serve as spiritual leader for our congregation. We expect our pastor to spend the equivalent of one workday a week away from the office in solitude devoted to spiritual renewal through prayer, Bible study, devotional reading, and journaling. The pastor will do no fund-raising; we do that ourselves. Our pastor will not manage our finances; while the pastor's vision will inform our financial priorities, we administer the budget. Our pastor will not take care of church facilities; we do that. Our pastor will not be responsible for the smooth operation of the church office; our administrative assistant sees to that. We will handle all administrative matters so you can give priority to prayer, to studying and meditating on Scripture, to teaching the Word, to counseling, and to building Christian community and equipping us for our ministries by giving priority to spending time with people.

Most churches expect their pastors to be their lead fund-raisers, but raising funds is not the pastor's calling.

Many pastors spend hours every week administering church finances, overseeing office operations, and caring for organizational tasks to keep the programs of the church running smoothly. Administration is essential to the life of the church, of course, which is why the Holy Spirit has given members of every church "gifts of administration" (1 Cor. 12:28 NIV). But administration is not central to the calling of pastors.

In *No Little Places* Ron Klassen writes of his first pastorate:

> I was taught a lot about church leadership in seminary. I was taught how to preach and how to guard my study hours, so I could preach my best. I was taught how to conduct services. I was taught how to lead meetings. I was taught how to administer. In short I was taught how to be a CEO.
>
> So when I started my first pastorate, I felt well-prepared to do all these things. I spent long hours in my study every week preparing sermons and as a result probably preached some of the best sermons the congregation had ever heard. I used the skills I had developed to make our worship services run more smoothly than ever before. I worked at administration, ensuring that every church event was organized to a *T*. I loved it all, and I did it well.
>
> Yet my ministry was going nowhere. People were sitting through my sermons and taking part in the events I organized, but I could see that these sermons and events weren't making much difference in people's lives. I was doing what I had been taught. Why wasn't it working?[1]

The typical church is suffering from a shortage of spiritual leadership—not because the pastor or pastors are not qualified to lead spiritually, but because they are so burdened with the work of institutional maintenance that they have little time to do what the church most needs them to do.

Minimize Administrative Tasks

Churches can free their pastors from these administrative tasks by hiring support staff or by reassigning such tasks to lay volunteers. These responsibilities fall primarily in five areas: office management, facility management, financial management, program management, and fund-raising.

Office Management

Euclid Baptist Church in Spokane, Washington, had two services, but the church still only had a part-time secretary. "Last week I needed to call a meeting for one evening," the pastor told me. "Our secretary wasn't in that morning, so I started calling around. I had trouble reaching people, and in the end still didn't get enough for a quorum, so I had to call people back and reschedule. In all I spent four hours just trying to call that one meeting." As I listened to him, he seemed to be climbing the walls because he wasn't free to spend his time doing what he knew he needed to be doing.

The pastor of a growing church of two hundred had only a half-time secretary. "Ken," I told him, "you need a full-time executive secretary."

His response was typical. "What would I ever do with a full-time secretary?"

I told him, "You're probably spending 25 to 40 percent of your time doing things a secretary could do as well as you or better," and I listed several examples. I then asked him to keep a log for two weeks of everything he did that a secretary could do at least as well as he could.

Here are some of the things I told him to watch for:

1. *Receiving visitors.* Ken was acting as receptionist when anyone came into the office during the time the secretary was gone.
2. *Answering the phone.* A secretary could receive all phone calls, and if fully informed, could personally handle 80 percent of them.
3. *Making calls.* A secretary could make many phone calls, such as calls to notify people of meetings.
4. *Producing communications.* A secretary can type form letters and the pastor's correspondence, learn to answer much of the church's correspondence, produce the church newsletter and bulletin, and much more. Euclid's half-time secretary was doing some but not all of these things.
5. *Keeping records.* A secretary can file and retrieve information.
6. *Schedule building use.* Usually in a small church, the secretary schedules the use of space and arranges with the custodian for setup and cleanup for each event.

Ken did end up hiring a full-time secretary.

Churches that have no secretary can sometimes literally double the time their pastors can invest in pastoring either by hiring a secretary or by filling the same need with reliable, informed lay volunteers.

Facility Management

At Colorado Springs First Church of the Nazarene, the pastoral staff spent more of the staff meeting time scheduling space than talking about people and ministries. The building was extremely busy, which was good, because it meant it was being used. But it also meant that scheduling became a major job.

Groups using the building were also responsible to set up their own rooms, which wasn't working well. People would often waste the first fifteen minutes of their meeting time setting up. I suggested the church hire a facilities manager to take care of building maintenance, to schedule the use of the building, and to set up for meetings. The church hired an excellent facilities manager, and overnight the staff members noticed a dramatic difference in how much time they had for ministry.

A Presbyterian church in the Oklahoma City area with three pastors on staff was considering adding another professional staff member. But the lead pastor was already handling so much administrative work that he was doing the equivalent of two full-time jobs, and I knew that adding another specialist for him to supervise would only add to his workload. His secretary, too, was doing the work of two people. I also noticed that after a meeting was held where food was served, the next morning secretaries and sometimes pastoral staff would be doing cleanup.

The last thing this church needed was another pastoral staff member. But I did recommend increasing staff in three areas: adding a business manager to take over one of the pastor's full-time jobs, including building management; strengthening the secretarial staff, including assigning an executive secretary exclusively to the pastor; and increasing the custodial staff so they could handle setup and tear-down.

In smaller churches the logistics are different, but the principle is the same: The people of the church should manage the facilities so the pastor doesn't have to. A secretary or volunteer can schedule use of the building, an active building committee can do or oversee maintenance, and a paid custodian or volunteers can clean, set up, and tear down.

Financial Management

A church in Brampton, Ontario, rewrote its pastor's job description to focus on only three areas: preaching, crisis visitation, and supporting the ministry of several lay pastors, each of whom would direct one area of the church's life. One of the lay pastors is responsible for the area of stewardship. This means, among other things, that the pastor no longer needs to attend finance committee meetings; they are handled by the lay pastor for stewardship.[2]

A church doesn't need to adopt Brampton's lay pastor structure to apply the same principle: The finance committee can and should assume responsibility for financial management without normally needing to involve the pastor in its business. Of course, the pastor will normally take the lead in setting forth the vision that shapes financial priorities and will approve the budget proposed by the finance committee.

Program Management

The Brampton church has lay pastors in many areas other than finances, including children's ministries, small groups, missions, outreach, visitation, and music. If a problem arises with a small group, for example, it is not taken to the professional pastor, but to the lay pastor for small groups. This happens in each area of the church's life. While part of the pastor's job is to select and then actively support these lay leaders, this church does not expect its pastor to personally administer any programs, and that gives him a freedom he has come to appreciate deeply.

Lay leadership of ministries within the church is nothing new, of course, but often lay leadership is seen as assisting or supplementing the pastor's administrative work. When a church relieves the pastor of all program administration duties, it allows the pastor to invest more time and energy in being a shepherd rather than a CEO.

Fund-Raising

Though it may come as a surprise to some pastors, many laypeople regard clergy with some degree of suspicion. Why? Because so much of what pastors do appears to be self-serving. Never is this truer than when pastors ask for money for the church.

Expecting pastors to be fund-raisers puts them in an almost impossible position. Because they are employed by the church, asking people to give more can look like they are trying to build their own businesses. And while it may not arouse suspicion for pastors to raise funds for causes outside the operation of the local church, often even this can be better handled by laypeople.

So how can we get our pastors out of the fund-raising business?

1. *Transfer fund-raising to the laity.* Lay leaders can go to the pastor and say, "We know it puts you in an awkward position to have to raise money to keep the church running. We would like to take responsibility for all the fund-raising so our people will have no reason to feel suspicious of you and so you can be free of that responsibility and able to invest your energy in what we hired you to do—be our spiritual leader."

Or pastors can initiate this change. When they are being interviewed by churches, they can say, "If I become your pastor, my job will not include fund-raising, administering the budget, managing the building, administering the church's programs, or managing the office. Those are all jobs that can be better done by the members of the church. I will gladly work with and support those who do these important jobs, but my call is not to be a CEO; my call is to pastor."

2. *Have laypeople teach biblical principles of financial management.* When Sally and I lived in McCall, Idaho, I taught a class like this in my local church using Larry Burkett's Bible study workbook, *How to Manage Your Money.* The purpose of this class wasn't to pound people with exhortations to give more. It was to teach the Bible's wonderfully practical wisdom about earning, spending, saving, and giving; wisdom that I knew could lead others to the same financial freedom Sally and I had discovered through this very kind of Bible study.

The most obvious result of this class was the greater financial freedom each family enjoyed as they brought their financial practices more in line with Scripture. A second result was an increase in giving made possible by the greater freedom families were experiencing. People didn't need to be "guilted" into giving more; they were eager to give more to support the ministries they believed in. They only needed to be shown how.

There was also a third benefit. Because almost every adult in the church eventually completed the study, they all brought similar understandings to church financial decisions. When the church was offered a property, for example, it was easy to decide against buying it since it would have meant going into debt, and the people were united in their commitment to avoid debt.

I recommend making a class on biblical principles of financial management—along with a class to acquaint people with the beliefs, goals, finances, and ministries of the church, and a class on spiritual gifts and personality types—part of the core curriculum every new member of the church completes when joining the church.

As people study biblical financial principles, they are better equipped to assume financial leadership. In McCall, Ralph and Sandy Turner, one of the couples in our first class on biblical finances, became the ones who would go before the congregation and explain how much our giving needed to increase for the church to be able to implement the ministries we were envisioning. Our pastor never had to do it.

Focus on Relationships

While pastors will always need to support and encourage those who handle the administrative tasks in the church, administrative work need not occupy much of any pastor's time. "The test of good management," management expert Peter Drucker tells pastors, "is that it enables you to be out of the office doing your real job." And what is the pastor's real job? Drucker writes: "The purpose, the mission, the objective of the minister is the person. The rest of it is important, perhaps, but it is strictly the side show. . . . The pastor is primarily a person available to other persons."[3]

I believe the pastor's work consists primarily of nurturing four kinds of relationships.

Relationships with Local Church Leaders

Paul writes that God called some to be "pastors and teachers, to equip the saints for the work of ministry" (Eph. 4:11–12). It is not the pastor's job to do the work of ministry for the church; rather, God calls pastors to equip all the believers to do the work of ministry. Pastors are not hired guns to do our work for us; they are player-coaches to train and guide us as we together do the work of the church.

Of course, one pastor cannot personally mentor everyone in a congregation. But one pastor can mentor a few who can in turn mentor others (2 Tim. 2:2). This was Jesus' strategy in the training of the Twelve. It was Paul's strategy.

No church in the New Testament was led by a single pastor; all were led by teams called by various names—prophets and teachers, apostles and elders. No one can effectively pastor a congregation alone; it takes a team. The wise pastor will, like Jesus and Paul, give high priority to building and nurturing a team of spiritual leaders who can together guide the life and work of the church.

Pastor Howard Chambers of Fairview Village Church did this with each member of his church board. Once or twice a month he would meet one-on-one with each board member, and they would report to each other on their spiritual lives and share prayer needs with each other. Howard then expected each of these board members to meet with another person in the church to repeat this process of "imprinting," as he called it. In this way he built a team of spiritually mature leaders within the church.

Relationships with Those in the Church

Ron Klassen tells what his experience in his first pastorate taught him.

What I learned was that my effectiveness as the pastor of the Brewster [Nebraska] church had little to do with how well I preached or led worship or administered, though those things all had their place. My effectiveness as pastor was determined primarily by my personal relationships with the people.

Effectiveness came only when I started spending less time in my study and more time in the local cafe drinking coffee. It came when I spent less time organizing church events and more time touring members' businesses or having lunch with them. It came when I got out of the office and went to ball games or went hunting. I learned that an hour of personal time with someone in my congregation could have more impact than a dozen sermons.[4]

Of course, in large congregations, the lead pastor cannot maintain a close relationship with every member. That's one reason building a team of spiritual leaders is so important; every church needs to have many people doing the work of pastoral care. But this immersion in the life of the congregation is essential for effective pastoral ministry.

This is true not only because one-on-one ministry is so powerful but also because pastors need this contact to keep their fingers on the pulses of their congregations. It keeps them attuned to the joys and sorrows, hurts and dreams of their people. Out of this sharing of life grow sermons that speak to people's real needs and a vision for the church that people will embrace.

Relationships with the Unchurched

Pastors must lead the way in building bridges to the unchurched. This does not mean churches hire pastors to do their evangelizing for them; rather, pastors are to be examples and equippers in doing outreach. Just as Jesus did much of his outreach with his disciples observing and sometimes participating, equipping pastors will not separate outreach from equipping but will teach others how to respond to all kinds of needs—spiritual, physical, social—by involving them in their own ministries to those outside the church.[5] These, in turn, can then equip still others through similar apprenticeships. In this way, ministering to the unchurched can become integrated into the daily life of entire congregations.

Relationship with God

When my writer, Eddy, was directing an inner city ministry, the ministry went through an especially stressful period, and he and his wife, Melody, found themselves wrestling with burnout. One of the ways they responded to that crisis was by renting a one-room apartment a few blocks from their home. They called it The Quiet Place.

Eddy began spending each Monday at The Quiet Place, where there was no phone and where no one knew how to reach him except his family and his secretary. He would use the day to journal, to take walks, to read the Bible or devotional books. He would pray by name for the people to whom he ministered, as well as for family and friends. He would seek God's guidance concerning decisions facing the ministry. If what he needed most to be renewed was rest, he would take a nap. Sometimes ideas for teaching or writing might come during this time, and if they did, he would jot them down. But he never went to The Quiet Place intending to prepare for teaching or to write an article. He blocked off office time for those tasks. The day had just one purpose—spiritual renewal.

Melody spent Fridays at The Quiet Place and used the time in the same way.

For both of them, spending one day a week in solitude for spiritual renewal proved to be a turning point. Neither had any doubt that their Quiet Place day had led to personal spiritual renewal and healing and to increased effectiveness in ministry.

Some time later they visited a pastor friend of theirs in New York City who was feeling overwhelmed by the demands of his work. When Eddy suggested he consider spending one day a week in solitude for spiritual renewal, he replied, "My board won't let me. I have to be in the office every day from eight to five. I can't even be away from the office on church business during office hours." Because of his board's expectations, not only was his spiritual life suffering but his family life was hurting as well. It wasn't long before he resigned that position.

Though I'm sure they don't mean to, many churches require so much from their pastors that it is almost impossible for them to spend the time they need in personal prayer and Bible study, praying for the people of the church, and seeking God's guidance for their ministry. But if we truly believe—as we claim to believe—that God's power, not human power, is what makes ministry happen, then these times are at the very heart of a pastor's work. Rather than making it hard for our pastors to take time for solitude and spiritual renewal, we ought to be requiring them to set aside one day a week—or whatever time frame works best for them—for uninterrupted time alone with God.

The Preacher-Scholar

Where are our pastors to find the time to spend on all these relationships—equipping leaders, staying in touch with the congregation, ministering personally to those outside the church, and setting aside a day or so each week for nurturing their personal relationships with God? Can all this time be freed up by reassigning the church's administrative work to support staff and lay volunteers?

In some cases, yes. But in other cases, further changes in the pastor's use of time will be needed.

I once heard a pastor promise, as he was being interviewed by a church board, that if he became their pastor, he would spend at least thirty hours a week in sermon preparation. And he did.

Ron Klassen tells how he was taught in seminary to spend more than twenty hours a week in sermon preparation, based on the belief that strong preaching was central to building a church.

This is what many seminaries are teaching. Pastors are being taught that they should spend twenty to thirty hours or more a week in sermon preparation, and they are being taught to function as CEOs. Pastors who follow this advice end up spending most of their working time in the church office doing administrative work and studying.

As important as it is for our pastors to be biblically informed, I do not believe that twenty to thirty hours a week of academic study is the best way for pastors to prepare sermons that have the power to change lives. I believe that if pastors will immerse themselves every week in the four relationships already described—discipling leaders, spending personal time with members of the congregation, reaching out in ministry to the unchurched, and spending time one-on-one with God—they will never be at a loss for sermon material. When a pastor is listening to God through prayer and Scripture and is in constant, close contact with people, it is not hard to identify what God has to say that speaks to people's needs.

Of course, preachers will still need to be careful scholars and will still need to spend time planning their sermons. But the ideas for the sermons will come not from reading books but from listening to the

Holy Spirit and to the lives of people. A pastor who prepares sermons this way will not need to spend twenty to thirty hours in academic study each week. For this pastor the time with God and with people provides sermon research far more valuable than any that can come from books. By the time the pastor sits down to outline a sermon, most of the sermon preparation has already been done.

Empowering Your Pastor

What does all this have to do with church finances? If a church is to move from institutionalism-driven spending to purpose-driven spending, this change of focus must occur in every area of church spending, including staffing. Freeing our pastors to focus on relational ministry rather than on institutional maintenance is essential to getting the maximum return on the money we invest in pastoral staff. More important, it is critical to the church's effectiveness in carrying out its mission.

It is impossible, of course, to define a single ideal for a pastor's time use that will fit every pastor or every church. A pastor whose strongest spiritual gift is evangelism, for example, should spend his or her time differently than one whose primary gift is teaching. As a church grows from fifty to two hundred and beyond, some aspects of a pastor's time use should, indeed must, change.

But every church can apply the principles outlined in this chapter: freeing pastors from as much administrative detail as possible, making it easy for pastors to give priority to personal spiritual renewal, and encouraging pastors to make personal relationships the heart of their ministries. The "Pastor's Time Use" inventory that follows is one tool that may help you to free your pastor for even greater effectiveness.

To find out what your church can do to free your pastor for pastoral ministry, make two copies of this inventory and give it to your pastor along with a copy of this book. Ask your pastor to return the completed inventories and dream job description to an appropriate member of the church board or lay leadership team for possible action.

Instructions to Pastor

1. Fill out the inventory to reflect your present use of time.
2. Read chapter 6 of this book, "Freeing Spiritual Leaders to Lead."
3. Answer the questions under "Your Dream Job Description."
4. Fill out the inventory a second time to reflect ideal time use.

Administration

Total the following six subcategories.

Building Management

- Scheduling the use of the building.
- Doing, supervising, and/or planning maintenance, improvements, construction, set-up and tear-down, grounds care, custodial work. Include time in meetings where these matters are being discussed.
- Relating to government agencies regarding permits, safety inspections, etc.

*Hours per week*_____

Office Management

- Receiving office visitors that could be received by qualified support staff.
- Taking phone calls that could be taken by qualified support staff.
- Handling/answering mail that could be handled by a qualified administrative assistant.
- Doing any kind of office work that a qualified secretary could do as well (typing, copying, filing, keeping records, mailings, etc.).

- Purchasing supplies, running office-related errands.

Hours per week _____

Financial Management

- Preparing budgets.
- Participation in finance committee meetings; that portion of other meetings, such as board meetings, where finances are the agenda; meeting with church treasurer or others concerning financial matters.
- Keeping financial records; monitoring income and spending.
- Getting bids or gathering other information concerning possible expenditures.
- Making deposits, paying bills, relating to lenders.

Hours per week _____

Program Management

- Planning and maintaining existing church programs, such as Sunday school, youth programs, vacation Bible school, including attending meetings where this is the agenda.
- Crisis management: dealing with problems that arise in church programs.
- Personally supervising any church program. (Do not include here activities whose primary purpose is equipping lay leaders for their ministries.)

Hours per week _____

Fund-Raising

- Preparing for and implementing a fund-raising campaign; include meeting time spent on this purpose.
- Contacting prospective donors by mail, phone, or in person to encourage giving.
- Special fund-raising events.

Hours per week _____

Other Administration

- Improving management skills.
- Relating to denominational or church agencies (reporting, attending conferences, serving on boards or committees).
- _____

Hours per week _____

Total hours per week _____

Study / Sermon Preparation

Include here all reading, study, course work, writing, practice delivery, etc., engaged in primarily to prepare to preach or teach. Do not include devotional activities engaged in primarily for personal growth or renewal.

Hours per week_____

Public Ministry

- Preaching and teaching (not including preparation).
- Attending the services, regular midweek activities, and other large group events put on by your church, such as concerts, Christmas programs, etc.
- Planning worship services, including coordination with other participants (musicians, etc.).
- Weddings and funerals, including preparation.
- Church events or activities where you have a leadership role (as opposed to being free to relate to people informally one-on-one).
- Participating as clergy in community events, such as giving invocations, sharing leadership in joint services, etc.

Hours per week_____

Equipping Leaders

Time spent one-on-one or in group settings where your primary purpose is to equip and support people for their ministries.

Hours per week_____

Personal Ministry to Those within the Church

- Counseling people in your church.
- Pastoral calls to people within the congregation.
- Time spent informally with members of the congregation—over a meal, at a ball game, etc.
- Time spent in a small group within your church where the primary purpose is building relationships of Christian community.

- Time at church social events where you spend most of your time relating to people in the church one-on-one.
- Phone calls, notes, cards, etc., intended primarily to nurture personal relationships with people within the church.

Hours per week _____

Ministry to Those outside the Church

- Counseling people outside your church.
- Pastoral calls to people not a part of the church.
- Follow-up of visitors to the church.
- Activities engaged in specifically to build relationships with unbelievers.
- Participation in group evangelism such as an evangelistic Bible study.
- Participation in ministries of intentional outreach such as prison ministry, providing

emergency financial assistance, offering recovery programs, sponsoring classes for those outside the church, etc.
- Doing intentional outreach.
- Participation in civic and community groups to build relationships with people outside the church.
- Serving on boards of community service and ministry organizations.

Hours per week _____

Personal Spiritual Renewal

Include here all time spent in devotional reading of Scripture or books, prayer, journaling, meeting with a spiritual director, attending retreats intended for your own personal renewal or spiritual growth (not those where you are in leadership), participation in a pastor's support group.

*Hours per week*_____

Other

Include here all other activities that are a regular part of your work. Itemize any that take significant time on a regular basis.

- _____
- _____
- _____
- _____
- _____
- _____

*Hours per week*_____

Totals

Administration (all six categories):		Ministry to those outside the church	_____
Study/sermon preparation	_____	Personal spiritual renewal	_____
Public ministry	_____	Other	_____
Equipping leaders	_____	Total Hours Per Week—All Tasks	_____
Personal ministry to those within the church	_____		

Your Dream Job Description

1.(a) On which aspects of your job description do you wish you could spend less time? Be specific.

   (b) What would it take to make it possible for you to spend less time on these? (For example, hiring support staff, lay volunteers, change in the congregation's expectations, acquiring new skills.)

2.(a) In what areas would you like to be able to spend more time? If you had more time for these areas, how would you use it?

   (b) What would need to happen for you to be able to devote more time to these areas?

3. What can your church board or leadership team do to make these changes possible? (For example, change your job description, change structures, hire support staff, recruit volunteers, etc.)

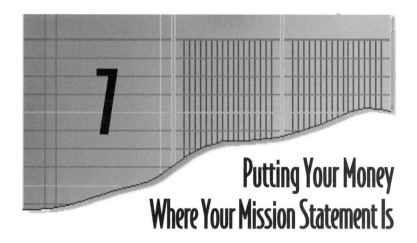

Putting Your Money
Where Your Mission Statement Is

"The church has gone astray, becoming an end in itself rather than a means to God's ends," writes Edward White of Alban Institute. "Preoccupied with its own survival, the church has become an institution."[1]

In churches where this is true, it shows up in the church's spending priorities. A church preoccupied with its own survival spends most of its money on its own institutional life. As Howard Snyder writes, "The church often betrays the kingdom of God . . . by consuming a disproportionate share of her resources on her own comfort and maintenance."[2] In contrast, a church strongly committed to serving not only its own members but those outside the church as well makes intentional outreach a top spending priority.

The chart on page 82 reflecting the spending of an actual Lutheran church is fairly typical of the spending priorities of North American churches today.

Where is this church putting more of its resources? A quick glance at the numbers shows that 88 percent of this church's money goes to maintaining its own life, while just 12 percent is given to others. Some of the staff, operations, and facilities budgets support ministries of intentional outreach, but in this church's case, as with most churches I've worked with, the percentage is small—not more than 2 or 3 percent.

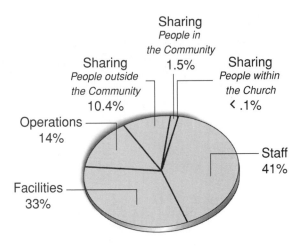

One church's budget priorities, fairly typical
of most North American churches.

The best single financial indicator of the priority a church gives to directly meeting people's needs is the combined total of the two local sharing categories—sharing with people in the body and sharing with people in the community. Only 1.6 percent of this church's budget goes to meeting these local needs—the kind of giving that can and often does involve personal ministry to those in financial need.

While this church is more outwardly focused than many and is therefore growing, it still puts most of its money—as well as time and energy—into maintaining its own structures and operating ministry programs for its own members. These things are not bad. In fact many of them are necessary. What is lacking is balance, balance between an inward and outward focus.

A church caught up in institutionalism is focused mostly on itself. The church motivated by a clear awareness of its mission will not just nurture its own members but will give equal priority to reaching out to others.

Purpose-Driven Spending

A church's budget can reveal institutionalism or it can show that the church is intent on its mission. What does a church's budget look like when the church is purpose driven, focused on serving the needs of people both within and outside the church?

How much a church spends on various purposes will, and should, vary depending on such factors as the size of the church, needs within the church body, level of giving, and availability of low-cost meeting

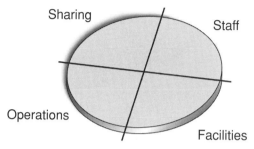

Quadrants of an "ideal" budget

space. Still, an "ideal" budget can serve as a useful guide, even though each church will have to adapt the ideal budget to its specific circumstances.

I suggest churches set a goal of spending one-fourth of their budgets in each of four areas: facilities, staff, operations, and sharing. For most churches this means spending a smaller percentage on facilities and staff, and a higher percentage on operations and sharing. The increased percentage for operations goes to expand ministries of outreach.

I further recommend that churches restructure staff job descriptions so that one-third of staff time is spent on intentional outreach, and that they set a goal of using their facilities for intentional outreach one-third of the time.

A church that gives 25 percent of its income to others (the total of all three sharing categories) and uses one-third of its staff, facility, and operations expenditures for ministries of intentional outreach will be spending half its income for sharing and outreach, and half on maintenance and nurture.

For a growing church of more than 250 with strong giving, this fifty-fifty balance is achievable. Smaller churches can move toward this goal as they grow.

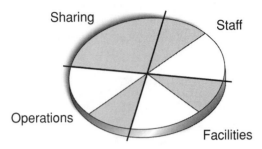

- ▨ Spending on needs of others
- ☐ Spending on our needs

A healthy 50-50 balance between spending
on our needs and the needs of others.

How can a church move from spending only 10 to 20 percent of its income on sharing and intentional outreach to spending as much as 50 percent on these purposes? In most cases, it calls for three major changes:

1. getting out of debt and staying out of debt;
2. radically reordering budget priorities; and
3. increasing per capita giving to 8 percent to 12 percent of household income.

Part 1 of this book described the first of these, how to become a debt-free church. This section of the book, part 2, deals with how to reorder budget priorities to invest more in sharing and intentional outreach. Part 3 will explain the third needed change—what can motivate the people of your church to give at the level needed to sustain outreach and growth.

To see how a church can shift from a typical budget to an ideal budget, let's consider the changes needed in each of the four budget quadrants—sharing, staff, operations, and facilities.

Quadrant I: Sharing

Not only was meeting the financial needs of people the highest financial priority of the New Testament church, but that priority was still largely intact at the time of the Reformation. John Calvin reflected the prevailing tradition of the time by advocating that one-fourth of all church income go to the poor in the congregation and one-fourth to others in need outside the church. Fully one-half of the church's income was to go to those in financial need.[3]

Most churches today spend less than 3 percent of their income on these two categories combined—a far cry from the 50 percent advocated by Calvin and what was probably an even higher percentage practiced by the New Testament church. Is it any wonder that so many non-Christians view today's church as just one more self-serving institution, another special interest group, rather than a community of faith that actively demonstrates mind-boggling love?

As a general rule, I recommend that a church budget 25 percent of its income for sharing and divide that amount approximately equally among the three sharing budget categories—giving to needs within the body, giving to needs in the community, and giving to needs outside the community. A church with many financial needs among its members may need to budget a higher percentage for this category. One with fewer needs of this kind will have more to give to people in need in the community.

A balance among the three sharing categories is essential to healthy outreach. While overseas missions is essential, when I see a church giving generously to overseas missions while giving little to meeting needs on its own doorstep, it makes me wonder: Is this church using check writing as a substitute for personal involvement in missions? Is it sending money to "the uttermost parts of the earth" while neglecting its Jerusalem, Judea, and Samaria?

Quadrant II: Staff

Most churches spend more than 25 percent of their budget on staffing, but seldom is it because they are overstaffed. In fact, understaffing is more common.

Of course, a church's size affects what percentage it spends on staffing. While larger churches usually hire one professional staff member for each 150–200 people in active attendance, many churches with fewer than 150 people have a full-time pastor. Because the smaller church has a lower people-to-pastor ratio, it typically spends more of its income for pastoral staff than the larger church does. In fact, small churches often spend 50 to 60 percent of their income on the pastor's salary and expenses.

So how would a church, like the church mentioned at the beginning of the chapter, reduce the percentage it spends on staff from 41 percent to 25 percent? It would probably not be by cutting staff. Here are some possibilities.

1. Hire support staff rather than professional staff. A growing church will often try to hire additional professional staff as quickly as possible. A more efficient use of staff is to make sure as much of the office work as possible is being handled by support staff. At a minimum the church should hire one full-time support staff for each two professional staff members. Some professional staff, including many senior pastors, will benefit from having a full-time support staff member assigned exclusively to them. Assigning as much office work as possible to support staff normally improves the quality of the office work and frees the professionals to devote more time to their ministries. This is usually a more cost-efficient way to extend professional staff than hiring additional professionals.

2. Empower nonprofessionals. If adequately supervised, office volunteers can do much of the work often done by paid staff. Also, much or even most of the pastoral work of the church can and should be done by nonprofessionals. The notion that churches are to hire professionals to be *the* ministers is clearly unbiblical; rather, all Christians are called to be ministers, and the special role of congregational leaders is to equip the rest of us to do the work of ministry (Eph. 4:11–12).

In churches with effective small group ministries with clearly defined leadership, most of the pastoral care can take place at the small group level. When professional staff give priority to equipping, supporting, and coordinating the ministries of nonprofessional pastors, fewer professionals are needed.

3. Increase giving. The reality is that most churches spend more than 25 percent on staffing because giving isn't strong enough to fully staff the church's ministries and still devote 75 percent of church income to other purposes. Most churches will need to increase giving to be able to adequately staff the church with 25 percent of their income.

Changing a church's focus from maintenance to mission also means changing the way staff time is used. An ambitious but reachable goal for most churches is for staff members to spend two-thirds of their time in ministry to the congregation and one-third of their time on ministries of intentional outreach. Chapter 6, "Freeing Spiritual Leaders to Lead," offers suggestions for helping churches achieve this goal.

Quadrant III: Operations

Operations includes two subcategories: church operations and office operations. Church operations include funds to operate all the church's ministry programs; office operations include all nonstaff funds for operating the church office. To sustain growth, most churches need to significantly increase spending in both areas, directing most of the increase to ministries of intentional outreach.

I was talking with one church committee about planning ministries of intentional outreach and told them, "Right now you don't have any of these. Everything you're doing is self-serving."

One person asked, "Are you telling us we are going to have to eliminate some of the things we are doing now that serve only us so we will have time and money for intentional outreach?"

"You got it," I answered. The group went on to identify several programs it could eliminate to free up resources for outreach.

Rather than having a single budget category called outreach, I recommend that each program area include a line item for intentional outreach. For example, the youth ministry budget would include a significant amount for outreach. If some of the youth in the youth group come from families who are not involved in church, some of this money could fund ministry to those families. The youth themselves could creatively plan how they want to reach out to their peers using these funds. If the church will adequately fund its youth ministry, the youth will then have time and energy to invest in intentional outreach, rather than having to wash cars to raise money. A huge plus to this approach: When the church provides funds and time and encouragement for the youth to reach out, the youth gain valuable experience in doing outreach.

Every Sunday school class can have a budget for intentional outreach. The senior adult ministry should have an intentional outreach budget. If the church operates a preschool, it should have a budget for intentional outreach to the families of the students. Every ministry program needs to designate a part of its budget for intentional outreach.

As the church adds new ministries of intentional outreach or adds outreach components to existing programs, that will cost money. As the ministry budgets increase, the office expenses to support those expanded ministries will also increase.

Of course, if the church staff is devoting one-third of its time to intentional outreach, it will be only natural for about one-third of the operations budget to be spent on ministries of intentional outreach as well.

Quadrant IV: Facilities

Churches that are spending more than 25 percent of their income on facilities can reduce that percentage by following the principles outlined in part 1 of this book—getting out of debt and staying out to eliminate all interest expense, and using buildings more creatively and intensively to sharply reduce the need for construction. As a general rule, smaller churches should avoid building until they grow to more than 150.

Even as a church works to reduce the percentage it spends on facilities, I recommend that it also reshape how it uses its facilities until it is using them for outreach one-third of the time.

Except for its office area, the typical church of a hundred or less normally uses its building no more than twelve hours a week, about 13 percent of daylight hours when the building could be used. If the facility is used for an outreach ministry two of those hours, the building use would break down something like this: maintenance and nurture, 11 percent; outreach, 2 percent; unused, 87 percent.

What would it take for such a building to be used for outreach one-third of the time?

1. Approach special events as intentional outreach. One church invested a tremendous amount of time, energy, and money in its Christmas program, Easter pageant, and Independence Day celebration. The church's leaders liked to think of these as outreach events. But when I asked,

"Do you get the names of the people who attend these events?" they told me they didn't. "Then you don't have any intention of following up on the unchurched people who come, do you?" I asked.

"I guess we don't," they answered. In this church's case these events were actually for themselves, not for others.

But by making one significant change, events like these can be used as effective outreach tools. The church needs to have a group of people, at least as large as the group putting on the performance, trained and ready to follow up on visitors.

2. Use your facility for weekday ministries. Charter Oak Methodist Church in Greensburg, Pennsylvania, provides facilities and utilities for a ministry of therapy for children, birth through age three, who have developmental disabilities. Monday through Friday the church provides the entire lower floor of the educational wing, including office and storage space. The same church has a day care center for three- and four-year-olds three days a week, serving families outside the church.

Many churches offer after-school latchkey programs, Mother's Day Out programs, and meeting space for support groups. A church in Bakersfield, California, has a weekly auto repair clinic in its parking lot where volunteers from the church do maintenance and minor repairs on cars without charging for their labor.

Just because a suitable facility is available, however, does not mean a particular ministry program should be started. There must be a real need for it. One church was considering starting a ministry to senior adults, so the pastor and I visited the senior center in town. It was thriving, offering a meal program, transportation, crafts—a full schedule of activities. I suggested that rather than trying to start their own program, the church support this excellent existing program with funds and volunteers.

Even a facility and a need are not enough reason to start a program. Before we start ministries, we must also have the ministers. Here we have finally come to the critical element. When there is a need and one or more called and gifted leaders are willing to respond to that need, only then is it time to develop a new ministry. When the need and called leaders are present, the facilities, the money, and other resources needed for the ministry will usually follow.

A church whose facilities are lying unused should look for ways to better use those facilities for ministry, but it should not let the facility shape the ministries. The vision for ministry should be shaped by a combination of people's needs and the availability of called leaders. If the church facility is useful for ministries conceived in this way, great. If these ministries don't need the church facility, that's fine too.

While it is good to offer the space to community groups or church-based programs that provide valuable services, using the building for intentional outreach means going a step further. For example, half of the students in a church-run preschool may come from outside the church, but if the church does nothing to reach out to minister to the families of those children, it's not really intentional outreach. Churches need to be intentional about using these programs to build bridges of ministry to unchurched people.

What percentage of the time is your church facility being used for maintenance and nurture? For intentional outreach? How much of the time is it empty or mostly empty? What are some steps your church could take to turn your facility into a more effective tool for ministry to your own people and for outreach to the community?

A church that has gotten bogged down in institutionalism can recover its sense of purpose. One sign of a renewed sense of purpose will be that people become a higher financial priority and institutional concerns a lower financial priority. If a church is intentionally reducing the proportion of its budget spent on facilities and staff, if it commits to increasing the amount it uses for sharing and outreach, if it is moving toward the goal of devoting to ministries of intentional outreach one-third of all staff time, one-third of all facility use, and one-third of all operations spending, that church is on its way from institutionalism to purpose. As it continues to close in on these goals, such a church will more and more be putting its money where its mission statement is.

Reality Check: Your Church's Budget Priorities

1. Total Spending

How much did your church spend for the year for all purposes (on and off budget spending)?

$_____

2. Spending Priorities

Divide your total spending for the year into the following categories. (See chapter 5 for category descriptions.) Then complete the pie graph to show the percentage spent for each area.

Sharing

With people
within the church $ _____ ___%

With people
in the community $ _____ ___%

With people
outside the community $ _____ ___%

Total sharing $ _____

Staff

Professional $ _____
Support $ _____
Total staff $ _____

_____ %

Operations

Church operations $ _____
Office operations $ _____
Total operations $ _____

_____ %

Facilities

Debt $ _____
Capital improvements $ _____
Building expenses $ _____
Total facilities $ _____

_____ %

3. Resources Used
for Intentional Outreach

(a) What percentage of church staff time is used for ministries of intentional outreach?*___%

(b) What percentage of the time are church facilities used for ministries of intentional outreach? ___%

4. How Balanced Is Your Spending?

How much of your church's spending goes for sharing and ministries of intentional outreach? How much goes for institutional maintenance and for ministries to members? To calculate this:

(a) List in the table on page 93 the total spending for each of the four categories.

(b) Enter the total sharing budget under the "Sharing/Intentional Outreach" column.

(c) Multiply the percentage of church staff time spent on intentional outreach (item 3a above) by total dollars spent on staff. Enter this amount on the "Staff" line under the "Sharing/Intentional Outreach" column. This is the portion of your staffing budget that goes for intentional outreach. Enter the balance of your staffing budget in the "Institutional Maintenance/Ministry to Members" column.

(d) Using the same percentage (from 3a), divide the total spent on operations in the same way. This assumes that the percentage of the operations budget used for ministries of intentional outreach will be approximately equivalent to the percentage of staff time used for intentional outreach.

---

* The Reality Check that follows chapter 6, "Pastor's Time Use," can be used to measure this. It can be modified for use with other church staff members.

(e) Multiply the percentage of the time church facilities are used for intentional outreach (from 4a) by your total facilities budget. Enter this amount on the "Facilities" line under the "Sharing/Intentional Outreach" column. Enter the balance of the facilities budget under the "Institutional Maintenance" column.

(f) Total both columns and calculate what percentage of your budget goes to each.

	Total	Sharing/ Intentional Outreach	Institutional Maintenance/ Ministry to Members
Sharing	_____	_____	
Staff	_____	_____	_____
Operations	_____	_____	_____
Facilities	_____	_____	_____
Totals	_____	_____	_____
Percent	100%	_____%	_____%

(g) Shade in those portions of your budget pie (p. 91) that go for sharing and intentional outreach—the entire sharing budget and those portions of the staff, operations, and facilities budgets used for intentional outreach.

(h) Evaluate. How balanced is your spending between sharing and intentional outreach on the one hand and institutional maintenance and ministry to members on the other? Are your spending priorities consistent with your church's mission statement?

From Insufficiency to Plenty

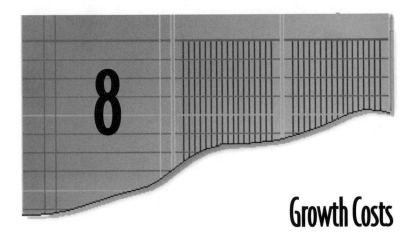

Growth Costs

When Pastor Brian Kelly of McLane Baptist Church just outside of Erie, Pennsylvania, called me, it was for the usual reasons. The church had outgrown its facilities and didn't know what to do next. They had already gone to double worship services. They were desperately short on parking. And the children's and adult Sunday school classes were overflowing the educational space.

For years the church had been debt-free and the people were strongly committed to keeping it that way. Without going into debt or taking funds away from ministry, where could the church find room to keep growing?

As Brian completed the church self-study in preparation for my consultation, he made a surprising discovery. As pressing as McLane's facility needs were, the church's most pressing need was not for facilities but for staff. Brian had come as pastor at a time when the congregation had dwindled to fewer than forty people and there was fear the church might not survive. In three years the church had grown to about two hundred but had not yet added an associate pastor. For the first time Brian understood why he was feeling so overwhelmed in his ministry.

But knowing he needed an associate didn't help much. The church's total budget was just over one hundred thousand dollars. He couldn't conceive of where the money for another professional staff member could come from.

During my consultation with McLane, I was able to outline a plan for modernizing and remodeling the facilities that would give the church room to double without new construction. And I confirmed Brian's realization that adding an associate pastor was already overdue. But where could the church get the money for these things?

As I analyzed the church's finances, I found that the sixty-four supporting giving units[1] were, on average, giving just 4 percent of their income to the church. I knew from working with other churches that a giving level of 3 percent is enough to sustain a nongrowing church. Nongrowing churches don't need to expand facilities, they don't need to add staff, and they don't need to spend money on intentional outreach. It doesn't take much money to keep a nongrowing church going.

For a church without debt to sustain modest growth, the giving level needs to be about 5 percent to 6 percent of the people's income. And to sustain growth of 10 percent or more a year, the people of the church need to be giving 8 percent to 12 percent of their income, depending on how extensive the church's facility needs are.

In fact, the faster new people are coming into the church, the greater the financial load the key financial supporters will need to carry. Why? Because people new to the church, especially those without a church background, are not usually strong givers at first. It typically takes about five years for a new member to develop the commitment and discipline to financially support the church as strongly as the long-time members do. So if a church doubles in size within a couple of years, the cost of operating the church will double, and the giving of those there before the growth spurt will need to double to cover the cost of growth, not to mention the spending needed to prepare for future growth.

McLane was a rapidly growing church with substantial facility needs. Four percent wasn't nearly enough to allow growth to continue at the same rate. In fact, the only reason the church had been able to grow rapidly for three years at that level of giving was that the church already owned debt-free a facility capable of handling a congregation of about two hundred.

But the church had reached the point where one of two things had to happen—either giving had to increase or growth had to stop. To keep growing, McLane would need to invest more in all four budget areas—staff, facilities, operations, and sharing.

Staff

A few months before I arrived for the consultation, McLane addressed their most urgent staff need: They hired a half-time secretary. I recommended the church immediately hire another part-time secretary. I also urged the church to hire another pastoral staff member within nine months.

As a general rule, a church needs one professional staff member for each 150 people. At the time of the consultation, McLane's Sunday worship attendance was averaging about 220. While Brian was clearly overextended, a key reason he had managed as well as he had without additional staff was because of the many strong lay leaders in the church. These included nine "care group" pastors who provided most of the pastoral care.

I usually recommend that the first associate added to a pastoral staff be a "minister of ministries," a person who can help the people of the church identify what ministries God has gifted and called them to do, see that they are equipped for those ministries, and support them in carrying them out. I urged McLane to hire such a person as soon as possible.

If the church had been ready to quit reaching out, they wouldn't have needed to hire an associate pastor. But to keep growing they would have to invest in more staff. Growth costs.

Facilities

While most churches considering new construction don't actually need to build, that doesn't mean they don't have facility needs. Some space needs can be met without spending money. McLane, for example, is moving some adult Christian education classes to Sunday evening to relieve Sunday morning overcrowding. But other changes do cost money. McLane needs to immediately expand parking lots, remodel the foyer, and buy new tables and chairs. This will cost about twenty-one thousand dollars. Before long the church will need to reroof the building and convert the parsonage into an administrative complex. All told, over the next few years the church will need to invest about one hundred thousand dollars in repairing and remodeling present facilities before it can start saving to build a multipurpose building.

While even nongrowing churches have to spend money to maintain their buildings, most of the money McLane needs to spend on facilities is to allow for growth. Growth costs.

Operations

As McLane's professional and support staffs expand, the office operations budget will need to increase correspondingly to support their work. Even more important, investment in ministry programs, especially those that focus on outreach and incorporating new people into the church, will need to increase.

McLane is working to strengthen this area in several ways. First, the church is developing a core curriculum for people new to the church. This is a two-year course of study that equips new members for full participation in the church's ministries. It consists of five classes on the following topics.

1. Introduction to McLane Baptist Church
2. Survey of the Bible
3. Biblical financial principles
4. Spiritual gifts and personality types
5. Accepting a ministry

Several of these classes call for curriculum, and that costs money.[2]

Some members of the church are laying the groundwork for launching a crisis hotline ministry. That ministry will take money.

One effective tool of outreach for McLane has been vacation Bible school. The church concludes the week with an outdoor service and cookout for the families of the children who attend. This year the church is making changes in that cookout to increase its effectiveness as an outreach event, changes that will mean spending twice as much on it as before.

There is no end to the creative ways money can be invested in effective ministries of intentional outreach. A Methodist church in Boise, Idaho, holds a special worship service for people with extreme allergies. Held in the chapel on a weekday, worshipers wear only natural fabrics and no perfume, makeup, or deodorant.

Trinity Methodist Church in downtown Denver has an after-work service on Thursdays. People come directly to the church after work where they eat a meal together and then have a worship service.

Advertising can reach new people, but most churches advertise ineffectively. Many churches don't even have a yellow pages listing or a get-acquainted brochure for visitors that describes the ways the church is available to minister to them. Churches that advertise in the paper or on the radio often advertise on the religion page or on Christian radio stations. That's okay, but if we're trying to reach unchurched people, those sources won't reach them. To reach unchurched people we need to advertise in the entertainment section of the newspaper and on the most popular rock station, country station, or talk radio station in town.

Whether we develop Mother's Day Out or Parents' Night Out programs, support groups, or an outreach counseling program, these ministries will take not only time and energy but money as well. Growth costs.

Sharing

Like many churches, McLane gives generously to missions far away (12 percent of the budget) but has been sharing far less with people in need in the community. In the year before the consultation, McLane spent just two-tenths of one percent of the budget to meet financial needs of people within the church.

To begin correcting this imbalance, the church has formed a committee to work with families in need. Not only does this committee provide direct financial assistance but it also works with families who need financial counseling and accountability to achieve financial stability. As this ministry develops, an increasing percentage of the church's budget will be invested in sharing with people in need, both within the church and in the community. Growth costs.

Paying for Growth

To fully fund these ministries, the people of the McClane church will need to increase their giving from 4 percent of their income to about 10 percent. To show how the church could reach this goal, I drew up a five-year financial plan based on increases of 1 ½ percent a year for two years (bringing giving to 5 ½ percent, then 7 percent) and an additional 1 percent for each of the following three years, resulting in 10 percent giving within five years. This five-year plan included enough funds to complete all the renovations and remodeling so that at the end of five years the church could start saving for the next major building program.

Evidently my proposal was too modest for the people of McLane. The congregation unanimously adopted a budget based on increasing giving not by 1 ½ percent, but by 2 percent, effective immediately. The church decided to immediately hire a second half-time secretary, to hire a full-time associate pastor in six months, and to invest twenty-one thousand dollars in facility improvements (primarily expanded parking) within nine months. After this vote Brian sent a short, low-key letter to the people of the church reporting the decision and asking each family to prayerfully consider increasing its giving to the church by 2 percent of its income.

Weekly giving immediately jumped, and it appears that giving for the year will exceed the ambitious budget the church adopted. Brian is confident that the church will complete its renovations and remodeling in far less than five years and so be ready to start saving sooner for the multipurpose building it is going to need to build. When the church does begin saving for this building, though, it won't be putting the money into a building fund but into a different kind of fund, one that reflects McLane's understanding of ministry.

No More Building Funds

Twenty years ago I never could have imagined saying this, but I no longer believe in church building funds. It's not that I don't believe a church should save for future facility needs; I urge churches to save the entire amount needed before building so they can build debt-free. The money being saved for building, however, shouldn't go into a building fund; it should go into what I call a growth fund. A Christian church in the San Francisco Bay area taught me the importance of this distinction.

The pastor of the church was nearing retirement and wanted to leave behind a new church building as the crowning achievement of his pastorate, so he hired an architect to draw up plans for the building of his dreams. Though the design was flamboyant and impractical, some in the congregation supported the pastor's dream and gave about two hundred thousand dollars to the building fund. Though this is a good bit of money, it was not nearly enough to start the building. Then the pastor died of a heart attack.

A young, energetic pastor was called to the church, and the church began to grow. They added a second service, creating the need for a fellowship foyer to handle the traffic between services. As the church grew, the staff also grew, to the point that the church needed to remodel the parsonage, converting it into an administrative center for the staff.

The congregation realized the building the former pastor had designed didn't fit the church's needs and never would, and that it would never be built. But when the pastor asked the building fund donors if they would release those designated funds so the church could use them to remodel, the donors refused. The wife of the former pastor, who was still active in the church, along with several of her friends, remained intent on building the unneeded building as a monument to the former pastor.

At the same time, because there was two hundred thousand dollars sitting in the building fund, the rest of the congregation wasn't motivated to give money to pay for the urgently needed remodeling. The pastor tried for five years to break this impasse before finally giving up and resigning.

This whole tragedy could have been avoided if the church had started a growth fund rather than a building fund. A church saves money for future facility needs in a growth fund, but with the understanding that the church can choose to use this fund in whatever ways best serve the needs of the church as it grows. A congregation might, for example, decide to plant a new church rather than to enlarge its facility, and the growth fund could help launch the new church. If the church should have an unexpected opportunity for intentional outreach or to respond to an emergency financial need in the church or community, it could turn to the growth fund. Setting aside money in a growth fund leaves the church free to invest that money wherever it is most needed to fund the continuing outreach and growth of the church, whether for facilities, staff, operations, or sharing.

Temple Bible Church in Temple, Texas, was a young, growing church meeting in rented facilities. They had purchased and paid for a property and raised most of the money needed to start building. Then a member of the church, a pilot, had a brain tumor and needed surgery. He was between jobs at the moment, so he had no health insurance. Without hesitation the church decided to use whatever church funds were needed to pay for his surgery. The church truly needed a building, but this member's needs came first.

Word of what the church was doing got out and money started coming in to help with the surgery, even from other states. In the end the donations received for the surgery replaced all the money taken from the building fund with two hundred dollars to spare. Though they didn't call it that, this church had a growth fund—a fund intended primarily to meet future facility needs but available to meet any other needs that might take priority. This church put the needs of people first and found that when they did, their need for facilities did not go unmet.

Inspiring People to Give

Money alone will not generate growth any more than fueling an airplane will in itself make a plane fly. But growth cannot continue for long unless giving increases to levels above those required for a nongrowing church. How can local church leaders succeed, as those at McLane Baptist are succeeding, in inspiring the people of the church to substantially increase how much they give? That is the subject of the next chapter.

Something Worth Giving To

Why do church attenders in North America give an average of only 3 percent to 4 percent of their income to the church, just about enough for the church to keep its doors open, to maintain the status quo? Why is it rare to find a church where the people give 8 percent to 12 percent of their income—the level needed to sustain vigorous growth and operate a variety of effective outreach ministries? Is it because people just basically don't like to give?

One church struggling to meet its budget surveyed its members to find out why they were giving less than expected. Here is a sample of their responses.

- "As it is, we basically say we will pay [our pastor] to minis-ter to us. We also value having a worship space. That is not enough of a direction. People give to things they believe in. If the money is not coming in, perhaps it is time to think about what this congregation is about."
- "I would give more. The problem is that there is no real need for a full-time pastor in this congregation, particularly since there is no real outward mission. I would rather support the agencies that are doing things I believe in."
- "To me it is a question of priorities. Over 90 percent of the budget is for internal things. The budget reflects a lack of congregational vision."

A major reason for the low level of giving in this church was not that people did not like to give; it was that they wanted their giving to count. Because the church had no clear sense of direction, because it had little vision for ministry, people were finding other places to give their money, places where they felt their giving would make a difference.

A generation ago many churches enjoyed strong financial support regardless of whether they had a clear direction or compelling vision. People gave out of a sense of institutional loyalty. Of course, some people still do, but Baby Boomers and Baby Busters are far less likely to give out of institutional loyalty than their parents and grandparents were.

The secret to inspiring people to give generously, even sacrificially, in today's church is to invite them to give not to an institution but to a vision. As we saw in the McLane church (chapter 8), when people believe something is worth giving to, they love to give.

Brian Kelly, pastor of the McLane church, understands the importance of focusing on the vision rather than on supporting the institution. "We always start by trying to determine what ministries God is calling us to do," he explains, "not with how much money we have. We don't say, 'We need this amount of money'; we say, 'This is the ministry God is calling us to do, and by the way, this is what it will cost.' The vision for ministry comes first, finances are secondary. When you commit to a ministry because you believe God is calling you to do it, God will provide the finances."

Develop a Plan and Stick with It

A mission statement alone cannot define the kind of vision that people love to give to. That mission statement must give birth to a plan, a plan made up of specific goals and specific steps to reach those goals.

A good master plan for a church has four parts: a ministry plan, a staffing plan, a financial plan, and a facilities plan. Of these the most important is the ministry plan, since the ministry plan should drive the other three components. Planning for staffing, finances, and facilities all should be shaped by what it will take to carry out the ministry plan.

As crucial as a long-term ministry plan is to a church's effectiveness, it is rare to find a church with a written ministry plan. Before I work for a church I always ask for a copy of their ministry plan. Churches have sent me many eloquent statements of purpose and good intentions, but in fifteen years of consulting work, I have yet to receive a single ministry plan with tangible goals and specific steps to reach those goals.

Nor is it enough to write up a ministry plan, or even to translate it into a staffing plan, facilities plan, and financial plan, though this is far more than most churches ever do. For a ministry plan to fulfill its purpose, the people of the church must commit to it for the long haul.

It is common for churches to experience a change of direction every three to five years, because on average that's how often churches change pastors, and each new pastor tends to start over with new goals. As Ron Klassen and John Koessler write, "Longtime members have seen pastor after pastor sweep in and pressure the congregation to adopt their ideas. After three or four or five years, they move on, leaving the churches to deal with the turmoil caused because they set significant changes in motion but left before seeing them through to completion."[1] That pattern is not the way to grow a church.

A ministry plan is not a once-for-all-time blueprint that never changes, but a living document. The church must keep updating and perfecting it, building and expanding on it. But it must not abandon it.

It is no accident that so many of the churches that have grown most consistently have had the same senior pastor, and in many cases the same core staff, for many years. Continuity of leadership has provided continuity of vision.

Though it is rare, it is possible for a growing church to change pastors without abandoning its ministry plan. I have seen it happen once. I give Gene Grate, the pastor who followed Woody Stevens at Colorado Springs First Nazarene, high marks for not coming in with an all-new ministry plan but taking the time to find out why the church was doing so well, improving on the existing ministry plan, and following through with the financial, facility, and staffing plans already in progress.

The Difference a Plan Makes

When we left Colorado Springs First Nazarene in chapter 2 (case study #3), the church was drowning in a sea of debt. Fortunately, the story doesn't end there. In 1990 church leaders implemented a visionary three-year plan that addressed the three areas around which this book is organized—debt, spending priorities, and giving. Central to all this was a ministry plan that involved working with members to identify their spiritual gifts and put those gifts to work in ministry.

The congregation responded enthusiastically to this vision, and the church's giving soared. Over the next three years the church was able to accelerate its mortgage payments, sharply reducing its indebtedness. The percentage of the budget invested in ministry increased as the church hired first an administrative pastor to coordinate ministries within the congregation, then a minister of evangelism to coordinate ministries of outreach.

As both attendance and giving shot up, the church was able to further expand its pastoral staff, bringing it to a level that could sustain growth. At the end of the three years, the debt, though still heavy, was no longer overwhelming, and the church was able to return to paying its regular mortgage payment, freeing more of its income for ministry.

The church updated its financial and facilities plans in 1993 and its ministry plan in 1994. Giving and attendance have continued to grow. From 1990 to 1995 worship attendance has doubled (from about 550 to 1100) and giving has approximately doubled.

Colorado Springs First Nazarene's story shows how a church that has made financial mistakes can take decisive steps to recover its freedom: by paying off debt; by making ministry, and especially outreach, a higher budget priority than facilities; and by increasing giving to support expanded ministries. The church is well on its way to freedom, but it is still suffering the consequences of its ten-year-old building debt. Most of the church's ministry programs are still underfunded, and the staff is not yet adequate for a congregation of eleven hundred.

I recently asked Kent Davis, the administrative pastor, "When will you have financial freedom?"

His answer: "When we make the last payment on the mortgage."

While the mortgage repayment schedule calls for five more years of payments, the church is once again accelerating its loan payments with the goal of achieving full financial freedom within three years.

For Colorado Springs First Nazarene the journey from financial bondage to financial freedom will end up taking thirteen years—thirteen tough years—but few if any of the eleven hundred people in the congregation would doubt that the journey has been worth taking. The church is experiencing its best days ever, with the promise of even greater freedom for ministry in the near future.

Motives for Giving

The unpopularity of sermons on giving is almost legendary. Is the resistance to such sermons simply because people are selfish, because they don't like to give? While selfish people certainly can be found even in the church, I suspect the primary problem lies elsewhere—in sermons that appeal mostly to motives of duty and obligation.

While feelings of guilt can motivate short-term responses, as a long-term motivator for giving, guilt is remarkably ineffective. In fact, negative motivations for giving are not even biblical. As a part of his biggest fund-raising effort, Paul wrote the Corinthians, "Each of you must give as you have made up your mind, not reluctantly or under compulsion, for God loves a cheerful giver" (2 Cor. 9:7). Paul certainly was not above scolding, but we never see him scolding to motivate people to give.

Colorado Springs First Nazarene and McLane Baptist are just two congregations that have been inspired to dramatically increase their regular giving levels, not because someone told them they ought to give but because the leaders in each church held up a compelling vision of what the church could be and do. People are eager to give, and give generously, because they believe in that vision.

I Have a Dream

I have a dream I'd like to share with you. Though it may strike some as an unrealistic fantasy, I see no reason it cannot become a reality. So far, though, I have not run across any church that has even tried it.

It is not unusual for a church to raise $1 million for a building program. It is a huge challenge for a church to raise such a sum, but every year a great many churches rise to that challenge.

As *When Not to Build* shows, most of these building programs are unnecessary; most churches can meet their space needs in better, less expensive ways. With that in mind, here's my dream.

What if a church would raise the same amount it would need for a major building program, not to build a building for itself but to fund ministries to hurting people primarily in their own community? What if the leadership team of the church were to spend several months dreaming about what the church could do with $1 million (or whatever a new building for the church would cost) to help the homeless, to support single parents, to provide counseling, to start support groups—to respond with compassion to the needs of people in and around the community?

What if the entire congregation were invited to help dream? What if serious research and planning were added to the dreaming to determine what it would take to turn the dreams into reality? What if the best of these dreams were presented to the congregation as a proposal for a massive Operation Outreach, and the people were challenged to give $1 million (or whatever a new building would cost them) to help make the dream a reality? As a way of investing money not in institutional maintenance but directly in the mission of the church? Can you imagine what would happen?

I believe people would give. People love to give to something bigger than themselves. Often all they need is the opportunity.

I wonder how often church building programs come about not because a church needs a building but because people have this need to give to something bigger than they are. I've seen it again and again: When the pastoral leaders in a congregation don't present a clear vision of the mission of the church, the laity will promote a building program as a substitute for that missing vision. The building program creates the illusion of significant ministry, even if the church doesn't need a building. But we don't have to settle for substitutes for mission; we can do the real thing.

What about your church? What would happen if your people had the chance to make an exciting, all-out, church-transforming outreach a reality through generously giving their time, energy, and money? Wouldn't you like to find out?

A lot of people don't get too excited about giving to institutions anymore, but they love to give to a vision. Why not challenge the people of your church with a vision for touching hurting people with Christ's love, a vision bigger than anything they have ever dreamed of? Give them something worth giving to. And watch them give.

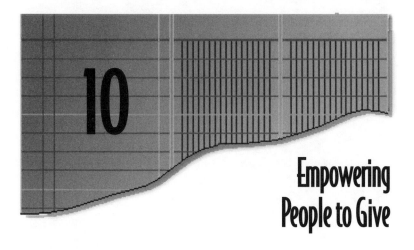

Empowering People to Give

People like to give when they see something worth giving to, but that alone doesn't make them able to give. What can a church do for its members who are willing but not able to give more because of heavy financial commitments?

A few years ago Ralph and Sandy Turner of McCall, Idaho, were in that very situation. "We gave our 10 percent tithe to the church," Sandy explains, "but we were so debt-ridden that if some other need came along and God asked us to give to it, we had nothing left to give."

Ralph and Sandy knew they were in financial trouble, so when their church offered a class in biblical financial principles, they eagerly signed up. During the first class session, as they read Scripture and filled out their Bible study workbook together, they experienced something new—unity in their family finances. "Because of our desire to obey God, our personal thoughts became secondary," Ralph remembers. "Our attitude was, if this is God's will as shown in the Scripture, whether we personally agree or disagree doesn't matter; we need to do it. And that gave us unity."

At the time, Ralph and Sandy were handling their finances according to what they call the world's financial system. "We were in debt up to our ears," Ralph explains, "buying places to rent so we could make more money. In most cases the income off those properties was less than the expenses. We were reaching into our pockets to make payments."

The Turners heard in class about the financial freedom that could come from being debt-free, and that made sense to them. "When we sat down at home and actually put on paper what we were spending on interest, we were amazed," Ralph says. "We could see that if we sold some of our properties and traded our big car in on a small car, our spendable income would increase by four thousand dollars a year. By the third week of class, we had sold a rental property and traded cars, eliminating fifty thousand dollars of debt. We didn't make any money on these sales, and that was okay because that wasn't our goal. Our goal was to get rid of a lot of frustration. The peace we felt was incredible."

Sandy remembers how people in the class told others in the church what was happening as they applied what they were learning. "I loved to see the excitement when someone told how, instead of running out and putting a new washing machine on the credit card, they trusted God to provide—and God provided. Or how God kept an old car running longer than expected when replacing it would have meant going into debt. God kept answering prayers and providing for the people in this class, and the excitement spread through the whole congregation. When it came time for the class to be offered again, people were waiting in line to take it."

As a result of this study, not only did the Turners set a goal of getting out of debt but they also resolved to adopt a moderate lifestyle. "As we understand it," Ralph says, "a moderate lifestyle is a personal matter between each family and God. It isn't doing everything you want to do, taking every vacation trip you'd like to take. But for us, neither has it meant living in poverty.

"As we worked on our budget, we would take it before the Lord and pray over it. Sometimes we would feel uncomfortable about certain items, and we would take that as the Holy Spirit's guidance to adjust these things. This didn't happen in just a week's time; we kept adjusting for a couple of years or so until we felt like our budget was where God wanted it to be."

When the Turners first set up a plan for becoming debt-free, they estimated it would take them four to six years to reach that goal. Unexpected developments made it possible for them to reach that goal in just two years. This enabled them to put their youngest child through college without borrowing. As Sandy says, "He went to school on the money we saved by not paying interest."

Freedom for the Church

The McCall church has gone on to offer this class on biblical financial principles regularly, and it has paid off for more than just the families that have taken it. "Now enough people have gone through these classes," Ralph says, "that it carries over to the church. There is now 100 percent agreement among our board members that our church will not go into debt. If the Lord wants us to do something, he will provide. If it is not provided now, we conclude that it must not be God's time."

"We haven't had one person in the congregation say to us, 'Please put us in debt for a new building,'" Sandy says. "It's been exactly the opposite. They say, 'Whatever you do, don't burden the church with debt.'"

This commitment has been put to the test repeatedly. When a house adjoining the church property came on the market, the church really needed the additional space the house could provide. At the same time, though, the church urgently needed to hire a half-time secretary to serve the needs of the growing congregation. The church chose to not go into debt for the property but to hire the secretary and increase the budgets of each of the church's individual ministries.

God honored that decision in a totally unexpected way. The owner of a house across the street offered to let the church use the house rent-free if they would just maintain it and pay the utilities. The church is still using that house today.

A couple of years later the house next door to the church came on the market again. The price was higher, but in the meantime the church had grown and giving had increased. Still committed to avoiding true debt,[1] the leaders of the church looked at their options. They didn't want to have to take pledges or special offerings. They came up instead with a plan they called "12 percent giving." They calculated that if the people of the church would increase their regular giving to 12 percent of their income, this, together with the rental income from the house, would meet all the church's ongoing needs, including the purchase of the property, without taking funds away from ministry. Lay leaders presented the plan to the church and the response was tremendous. Sandy recalls, "People were thrilled with the opportunity to give more."

For some who had never tithed before, 12 percent seemed totally out of reach. Ralph and Sandy would tell them, "If you can't give 12 percent now, try to give 1 or 2 percent more than you're giving now." Some started out by giving just 2 percent. When they found that to be pretty easy, they increased it to 3 percent, and they've kept increasing it by 1 percent at a time.

The church's commitment to avoid debt has also been tested by crowded worship services. Over the past eleven years, the McCall church has grown from twenty to two hundred. With their auditorium filling up, the church considered building on a new site. "We went out and looked at the property," Ralph says. "It would have been a beautiful location for us. But as we prayed about it, we realized that if we did this, our ministries would suffer."

The church kept growing and the option of relocating to build came up again. Again the board considered relocating but came to the same conclusion: Building would take money away from ministry. So rather than building, the church went to double worship services.

Ralph and Sandy now teach their church's class on biblical financial principles. They offer it not only to new members but also as a refresher course for those who have taken it before. Sandy says, "Every time we teach this class, there is always an immediate increase in giving to the church from the people who are taking it."

The class's purpose, of course, is not to pressure people to give more to the church; it is to help church families enjoy the financial freedom God wants for them. But a natural result of financial freedom is that people can give more to ministry.

Three Kinds of Giving

I recommend that every church offer a class on biblical financial principles, both for its members and as part of its core curriculum for new members. This class should cover not only what the Bible teaches about debt and a moderate lifestyle but also what it teaches about giving.

Though the Bible mentions many kinds of gifts, I'd like to highlight the three kinds of giving that I believe are most important for the people of our churches to understand today: regular percentage giving, giving out of surplus, and giving out of sacrifice.

Regular Percentage Giving

The best-known biblical example of proportional giving is tithing—the giving of a tenth. The spiritual principle behind tithing is worship, acknowledging God as God, as the provider and owner of all we have. According to Deuteronomy 14:23, tithing is "so that you may learn to fear the LORD your God always."

Though Hebrew scholars do not all agree, the Israelites may have paid a second tithe, at least every third year, and the Jewish historian Josephus writes that even a third tithe was collected.[2]

Tithing brought God's blessing. Malachi wrote, "Bring the full tithe into the storehouse, so that there may be food in my house, and thus put me to the test, says the LORD of hosts; see if I will not open the windows of heaven for you and pour down for you an overflowing blessing" (Mal. 3:10). Many Christians who tithe testify to its bringing God's blessing in their lives.

While we have no record of the New Testament church practicing tithing,[3] Paul did urge regular proportional giving: "On the first day of every week, each one of you should set aside a sum of money in keeping with his income" (1 Cor. 16:2 NIV). I believe that regular proportional giving is still God's primary plan for funding the work of the church.

Occasionally when I am working with a church, someone objects that tithing is an Old Testament practice, one not required of Christians. I never argue with that. I simply point out that in my experience, for a growing church to fully fund its ministries, all its members need to be giving in the range of 8 to 12 percent of their income.

Giving Out of Surplus

Giving out of surplus is based on the spiritual principle of contentment. People who are always wanting more, who never feel like they have enough, never think they have a surplus. But once members of a family prayerfully determine what is enough for them and establish a moderate lifestyle, they can recognize a surplus when God gives it. Paul referred to giving out of surplus as a way to share with fellow Christians with specific needs (2 Cor. 8:13–15).

Shortly after my writer, Eddy, was married he took a job as a carpenter's helper for $3.00 an hour. When they wrote out their budget, he and his wife could see no way to cover their basic expenses on that income. Familiar with the concept of giving out of surplus, they decided to give God the opportunity to give them a surplus if he wanted to. They promised God that if he provided a surplus—which in this case they defined as any income above basic living expenses—they would give half of the surplus to ministry.

During the three months Eddy held that job, God didn't increase their income, but he did come up with some creative ways of holding down their expenses. For example, as the time approached for them to buy car tags and renew their car insurance, they weren't sure how they would pay these bills. As it turned out they never had to, because before the bills came due, their car burned and their pastor loaned them an old car he was no longer using.

At the end of three months, Eddy and Melody added up how much surplus God had provided on $3.00 an hour: It came to $300.00. During those months, they had been able to give $150.00 out of surplus in addition to their regular percentage giving.

Giving Out of Sacrifice

Giving out of sacrifice either grows out of the spiritual principle of contentment or the principle of trust, depending on what kind of sacrifice is meant.

One meaning of sacrifice is to give up one thing for the sake of something of greater value. Once Sally and I were saving money for something we wanted, something good, but then felt God wanted us to use that money to meet the need of another person. Giving up something we wanted for the sake of something more important was a form of sacrifice made possible by contentment. Though we would have enjoyed what we were hoping to buy, we were content without it.

Another form of giving out of sacrifice that is rare among affluent people but common among those who are poor is giving away resources needed to meet basic needs. The widow who put her last two coins into the temple treasury was giving out of sacrifice (Mark 12:42; Luke 21:2). Paul reports how the churches of Macedonia, in spite of their "extreme poverty . . . overflowed in a wealth of generosity," giving "according to their means, and even beyond their means" because they wanted "the privilege of sharing in this ministry" (2 Cor. 8:2–4). How could the Macedonians have given beyond their means? By giving away even the money they needed for their own basic living expenses.

Why would they dare to give away money they needed for basic necessities? Because of their trust in God's provision. Paul goes on to say, "And God is able to provide you with every blessing in abundance, so that by always having enough of everything, you may share abundantly in every good work" (2 Cor. 9:8). Notice that Paul isn't just saying that God will provide our needs; he is saying that knowing that God is going to provide our needs makes it possible for us to "share abundantly in every good work."

We don't have to make sure our own needs are met first, then give what is left over to God. We can give first to "every good work," or as Jesus said, seek first the kingdom of God, with the confidence that God will give us everything we need.

Once when our daughter Cindy was wondering how she was going to stretch her grocery money until payday, she felt strongly impressed to go buy a bag of groceries for a specific family and take it to them. Her husband, Steve, was at work, and she didn't have a chance to discuss it with him, but she felt so strongly that she should do this and do it right away that she went ahead and did it. Sure enough, the woman to whom she gave the groceries was in urgent need and the groceries had come at a perfect time.

On the way home Cindy began worrying about how she would explain to Steve that she had spent all their grocery money on someone else. She was saved the explanation because before Steve got home, there was a knock at their door. Cindy opened the door to find an embarrassed friend from church who said, "I don't know what this is all about, but a while ago I felt the Lord was telling me to buy you groceries and bring them to you." She then brought in two or three times as many groceries as those Cindy had just given away.

Giving out of sacrifice means giving away something we need for our basic living expenses because of the confidence that when God has directed such giving, he has already promised to supply our needs.

Ending the Fuel Shortage

Most churches today are underfueled. They have far less income than they need to meet needs within their own church families and to reach out with love and power to the many hurting people in their communities. But this can change. How?

1. *Recognize that the church is underfueled.* Some churches that are underfunded know it. Many others, whose income runs about 3 to 4 percent of the members' income, accept this as normal. They don't realize that a church can begin growing with this level of income but that a much higher level of income, in the range of 8 to 12 percent giving, is needed to sustain effective outreach and vigorous growth.

2. *Give people something worth giving to.* More giving alone will not generate growth or greater outreach. In fact, giving more to an ingrown church may simply result in higher spending on institutional maintenance. For increased giving to lead to greater ministry, the vision needs to come first.

   But when people within the church have clearly identified how God is calling them to minister to hurting people, and the church is supporting those calls and inviting its members to give in response to them, people will count it a privilege to participate in turning those visions into reality through their giving.

3. *Teach biblical financial principles to every church family.* Wanting to give generously is not enough; God's people must also be able to give generously. This comes about when people experience the financial freedom that comes from applying biblical financial principles to their personal finances. Along with this freedom can come a greater joy in giving as Christians worship, acknowledging God's ownership through regular percentage giving, as contentment leads to giving out of surplus, and as trust in God's provision inspires occasional giving even of those resources needed for basic living expenses—giving out of sacrifice.

When God's people practice regular percentage giving, giving out of surplus, and giving out of sacrifice, God's work will never be crippled by lack of funds.

Ask your church treasurer to list the amount given by each giving unit during the year. A giving unit is a person or family whose giving is of record. Do not include large one-time gifts.

Significant Giving Units

Those giving more than $500

Number of significant
giving units $_____

Total giving of these units $_____

Average giving per unit
(total giving ÷
# of units) $_____

Giving $500 or more to any cause indicates a significant commitment to that cause. In most churches it takes all of these giving units to finance the ministry.

Supporting Giving Units

Those giving less than $500

Number of supporting
giving units   _____

Total giving of these units $_____

Average giving per unit
(total giving ÷
# of units)   _____

These gifts are important, but they will not drive the work of the church. Some of these will become significant givers when they catch a vision of the ministry of the church and become involved in it.

Percent-of-Income Giving

Find out the average household income for your community. Sources for this information are city or county planning departments, the library, or your chamber of commerce. Adjust this amount to reflect your congregation's income level. If your people have more income than the average family in the community, adjust it upward; if less, downward. A survey of the income levels of your significant giving units would be more accurate. See the sample survey form following this Reality Check. (Some churches prefer not to make such a survey.)

Average giving per significant giving unit divided by the average income equals the average percent of income given by your significant giving units.

Average giving: $ _____

÷ Average income: $ _____

                         = _____ %
                           of income
                           giving

This percentage is a strong indicator of your givers' current commitment.

Financial Survey of Givers
Do not sign your name—please.

This information will enable the finance committee to understand the giving patterns of our church family. This information will be used to develop a financial plan for the long-term growth of the congregation and our ministries.

For calendar year: _____

1. Gross income $_____

2. Total giving to our church $_____

3. Giving as percentage of income
   (giving divided by income)   _____%

4. Total giving to other than our church $_____

5. Additional giving will be required for the
   continued growth of our church. Would
   you be willing to increase your percentage-
   of-income giving to provide for these needs?   ___Yes ___No

If yes, would you indicate a percentage of income?   _____%

If no, please suggest how you think our church's
growth and facility needs should be financed.

_____

_____

_____

Thank you for your help,

Chairperson of Finance Committee

Conclusion

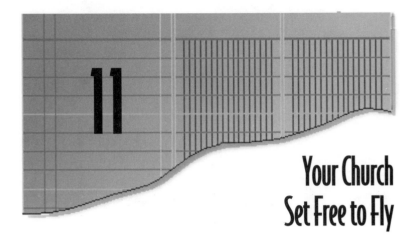

Your Church Set Free to Fly

I'd like you to dream a bit, exercise your imagination. Imagine for a moment that effective immediately your church is debt-free. You have no more mortgage payments to make. Imagine too that starting today, your church's regular income is triple what it has been. Your income is higher, your expenses lower, and the entire increase in your spendable income—more than two-thirds of your budget—is available for the church to invest in new or expanded ministry to people.

How will you use the money?

A few churches have received windfalls like this, and when they have, they have usually spent most of the money on buildings. Why?

That's the easiest way for a church to use up a lot of money.

But notice your instructions: Your church's increase in spendable income is available only for *new or expanded ministry to people*, not for institutional maintenance. That doesn't rule out spending some of it on facilities, but it does mean that it can be spent on facilities only if those facilities are truly necessary for your new or expanded ministries to people. Building to avoid going to double or triple worship services, for example, would not qualify. Remodeling an apartment building to convert it into a church-operated shelter for homeless families would qualify. Likewise, increasing your pastor's expense account so he can drive a luxury car wouldn't qualify; budgeting to pay salaries for the staff of the family shelter you will open would qualify.

Imagine first what you would do to better meet the financial needs of people within your own church. What could you do to make sure the church is aware of financial needs created by illness, accidents, unemployment, underemployment, separation or divorce, counseling expenses, caring for extended family, the breakdown of vehicles or appliances, or lack of economic opportunity? To whose attention will these needs be brought? Who will determine how the church can best respond to these needs, not only financially but with comfort, encouragement, counseling, teaching, accountability—whatever the situation calls for? How will your church get from where it is now to fulfilling the New Testament standard of no unmet financial need within the body?

Imagine next what ministries of intentional outreach your church could launch or expand, serving the people of your community. What training could you offer the people of your church to equip them to reach out more effectively? What visions for ministry have been lying dormant among various members of the church that could come to life with just the right staff and financial support? What worthwhile ministries are already operating in your community that could be made more effective, perhaps many times more effective, with the infusion of significant funds along with the personal involvement of people from your church?

As you envision new and expanded ministries, keep in mind that the most critical element in starting or expanding a ministry is not funding or facilities but leadership. Don't try to envision something that might be nice but that no one has an interest in leading; look first for where effective leadership is already in place or where someone may be sensing a call to give leadership to a new ministry. Then ask, How could we empower these leaders through new or expanded funding for their ministries?

Consider inviting the whole church to dream with you. Ask the members of your church, "What would you dream of doing to serve God and others if you had unlimited funds?" Their dreams taken together can shape the church's dreams.

Don't think small. Don't just think more of the same. Think big. Think creative. Think anything is possible.

Depending on the size of your church, you may come up with dozens of new possibilities for ministries of intentional outreach, or you may come up with hundreds. But don't stop dreaming, don't stop brainstorming, until you've come up with so many possibilities that pursuing even a fraction of the dreams would be enough to set your church on fire.

Finally, think creatively about ministering to people far away. Most churches I work with already give generously to overseas missions, and you may not need to increase the amount or percentage you invest in this area. But often such giving, while generous, is impersonal. There is little personal connection between the giver and the ministry to which the money is given.

Look for ways to increase the personal connection. Perhaps your church could adopt a mission family. Have the family visit the church and talk about their work whenever they are on furlough. Post the family's newsletters on the church bulletin board and reprint highlights in the church newsletter. You could write to the family and send cards or small gifts on the children's birthdays. Perhaps volunteers from your church could do short-term work on that mission field. (If you do this, take care to structure the experience so volunteers' work is truly empowering; poorly designed volunteer experiences can disempower the very people you are trying to serve.)

Keep dreaming until you have come up with constructive ways to invest all the increase in spendable income made possible by eliminating your debt and tripling your giving. Invest it to meet needs within your own church family, invest it in intentional local outreach, invest it in ministry to people far away.

Then lean back and take a look at what you've dreamed up. How would you like to be a part of that kind of church? If you care about introducing people to Christ, if you care about touching the lives of hurting people with God's love, I already know your answer to that question: You'd love it!

But it's only a fantasy. I asked you to fantasize about what could happen if your church were suddenly debt-free and giving tripled overnight. And that simply won't happen.

But if you don't believe that the unconventional financial wisdom outlined in the previous ten chapters is just pie in the sky, if you believe it works for real churches in real life, then you also know that your dream church is not as unrealistic as some people might think. In fact the only part of your dream that is inherently unrealistic is the time frame. It can't happen overnight, but it can happen.

From part 1, "From Indebtedness to Provision," you know that a church can get out of debt and stay out of debt, even through a major building program. It may take five years or ten or even thirteen, as with Colorado Springs First Nazarene, but it can be done.

From part 3, "From Insufficiency to Plenty," you know that a congregation can triple its regular giving from the usual rate of 3 to 4 percent of its income to 10 to 12 percent. This can happen only when the people have an inspiring vision to give to and when they have been equipped to better manage their personal finances through practical training. And it can only take place over a period of years during which the people increase their percentage-of-income giving by 1 percent, or perhaps 2 percent, a year. But when all these things happen, most churches can, over a period of five to seven years, empower their people to give three times as much to the ministries of the church.

The key to all this happening, though, isn't dollars and cents; the key is a passion for ministry. A church that gets out of debt and triples its giving but does not have a passion for ministry will not minister more effectively; in all likelihood it will simply pour more and more money into institutional maintenance, especially buildings.

That is why the message of part 2, "From Institutionalism to Purpose," is at the heart of this unconventional financial wisdom. By itself, no amount of financial expertise can make your church's ministries more effective. But if it is a passion for ministry to people that inspires you to do whatever it takes to get out of debt and multiply your giving, the kind of church you have been dreaming of can happen.

No longer overloaded, no longer underfueled, no longer off course, your church can be set free to fly.

Dare to dream of the potential waiting to be unleashed in your church! Assume that all of you have decided to make the commitment of ministry and money to fulfill the dream.

Your Potential Giving

Assume a 10 percent giving level by the significant giving units and add all other current giving to this amount.

Total of potential giving $_____

Your Potential Priorities

If your church had this amount of income, what would you want your spending priorities to be? Using the "ideal budget pie" as a guide, adapt the percentages to your church's needs, opportunities, and vision. Allocate your total potential giving among the six categories on page 131 in a way that expresses the financial priorities you would like to see your church have.

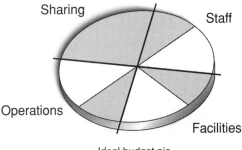

■ Spending on needs of others
□ Spending on our needs

Sharing

Staff

Operations

Facilities

Ideal budget pie

Sharing

With people
  within the church $ _____ ___%

With people
  in the community $ _____ ___%

With people
  outside the community $ _____ ___%

Total sharing $ _____

Staff

$ _____
        ___%

Operations

$ _____
      ___%

Facilities

$ _____
      ___%

Getting There from Here

1. What percentage of their income are your significant giving units now giving to the church? (Get this figure from "Reality Check: Your Church's Giving" following chapter 10.) _____%

2. If these givers would increase their giving by 1 percent of income each year, how many years would it take for their giving to average 10 percent of income? (Example: Average giving is 3 percent; it would take 7 years of 1 percent increase per year.) _____ years

3. Estimate what your yearly giving income would be during each year of this increase.

   Year _____ _____ _____ _____ _____ _____ _____

   Giving _____ _____ _____ _____ _____ _____ _____

4. Prepare an outline budget for each of these years, allocating funds to each of the six budget categories. As a basis for budgeting, for each year project (1) attendance, (2) staff needs (professional and support), (3) facility needs, and (4) vision for ministry.

   If you are serious about implementing this kind of plan, involve your leadership team in preparing such a budget for the next several years, showing how your church can, within a few years, fulfill its giving potential. Focus on vision for ministry. How will the church use this increased giving to increase its ministry, particularly in the areas of sharing and intentional outreach?

5. Once your leadership team is united behind this vision, present it to the congregation. Use a pie graph to show how giving dollars are now being spent. Use a second pie graph to show how the increase will be used. Describe what people needs will be met, what outreach will be accomplished, what staff will be provided, and what facility needs will be met (including debt to be paid or "growth fund" if there is no debt). Present both your short-range plan (next year) and your long-range plan.

6. Give your people an opportunity to respond. Ask all givers to fill out the financial survey (see end of chapter 10), inviting them to consider increasing their percentage-of-income giving for the coming year.

   Note: If special offerings for missions are a meaningful form of giving for your people, by all means continue them. Be sure, however, to include in this giving all three parts of the sharing budget—intentional meeting of needs of people within the body, people in the community, and people outside the community. This giving can be in addition to the basic percentage-of-income giving, and you can modify your financial survey form to reflect this.

7. Repeat this process each year: Review last year's finances, share your short-term and long-term vision, and invite renewed commitment using financial survey forms.

8. Rejoice as your church fulfills its ministry potential!

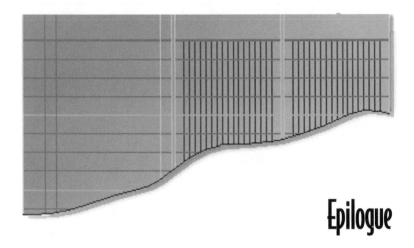

Epilogue

Just as we were finishing the writing of this book, our neighbor Fran told me the following story, which underscored for me why this book needed to be written.

Bob and I were married on a Saturday morning in our church's beautiful new four-thousand-seat sanctuary, surrounded by friends and family. After the wedding we drove seventy miles to the hotel where we were staying for two nights before leaving on our honeymoon.

Normally we would not have retraced the seventy miles to our church the next morning, but I had the chance to join the church that Sunday. What a perfect time, I thought, to invite several non-Christian family members to worship with us, family members who had come in for our wedding, family members who rarely heard the gospel! And where better to invite them than to a church with a century-old tradition of emphasizing missions and evangelism?

That morning I stood and celebrated with twenty-five others who were also joining the church, many of whom had invited their unchurched family members and friends to share the occasion with them too. Then I returned to my seat where Bob and I were surrounded by family—my daughter, my two brothers, my adoptive parents, and two of Bob's relatives.

Eventually the moment I had been waiting for arrived—the time for the sermon. But rather than preaching, the pastor asked one of the church officers to speak. This layman stood and proceeded to scold the congregation for not keeping up with the pledges they had made to pay the debt on the new building. I fidgeted, glancing at my adoptive father who had often complained that "all churches ever talk about is money." I knew how he felt; I had felt exactly the same way before I became a Christian.

After a twenty-minute tongue-lashing, the church officer finally sat down, but that wasn't the end of it. Next the pastor got up and basically repeated everything the first man had said. The service ended without the gospel ever being preached.

Bob and I were humiliated and, the moment the service was over, apologized profusely to our guests, but nothing we could say could undo the damage. My father reminded us that, sure enough, "all they ever talk about is money." This happened six and a half years ago, and he has not once been back inside a church, nor have several of our other relatives who were with us that day.

The way a church approaches money has eternal consequences. As Fran's story shows, church finances, wrongly handled, can alienate people from the church and ultimately from God.

But as many other stories in these pages have shown, a wise, creative approach to church finances can enhance a church's ability to build Christian community, equip believers for ministry, and mobilize members to reach out to hurting people with God's love.

My prayer is that as your church applies the unconventional financial wisdom about which you have read, you will enjoy a greater freedom to minister than you have ever known before, a freedom that will bear eternal fruit.

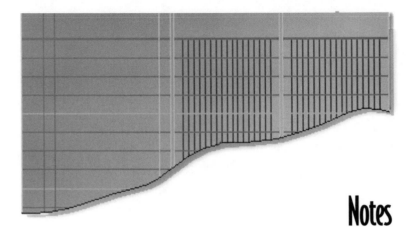

Notes

Introduction

1. Ray Bowman with Eddy Hall, *When Not to Build: An Architect's Unconventional Wisdom for the Growing Church* (Grand Rapids: Baker, 1992).

Chapter 1: Confessions of a Borrow-and-Build Promoter

1. Larry Burkett, *How to Manage Your Money: An In-Depth Bible Study on Personal Finances* (Chicago: Moody, 1991). Larry Burkett is president of Christian Financial Concepts.

Chapter 2: Selling the Church's Birthright

1. Throughout this book, names of congregations and pastors have been changed except when the town where the church is located is named.

2. Romans 13:8, "Owe no one anything, except to love one another," has sometimes been interpreted to forbid Christians from borrowing. The context, however, does not suggest that Paul's topic is borrowing. Rather, the passage refers to faithfully fulfilling both financial and nonfinancial obligations (cf. 13:6).

3. For a full discussion of how to tell if a church needs to build and what alternatives to building may better meet a growing church's needs for space, see our book *When Not to Build: An Archi-*

tect's Unconventional Wisdom for the Growing Church (Grand Rapids: Baker, 1992).

Chapter 3: Hidden Costs of Debt

1. Randy C. Alcorn, *Money, Possessions and Eternity* (Wheaton: Tyndale House, 1989), 326–27.

2. While it takes longer—four to seven years—for larger churches to move to a cell-based structure, many churches are successfully making that transition. While churches usually adopt the cell-based model primarily for ministry reasons, not facility reasons, spending less on facilities does enable them to invest more in ministry and almost certainly contributes to the rapid growth of many cell churches.

An excellent book on what a cell church is and how an existing congregation can become a cell church is William A. Beckham's *The Second Reformation: Reshaping the Church for the 21st Century* (Houston: Touch Publications, 1995). Many resources for cell churches—books, curriculum, videos, training events, etc.—are available through Touch Outreach Ministries, Inc., P. O. Box 19888, Houston, TX 77224, phone 1-800-735-5865.

Chapter 5: The Trap of Institutionalism

1. Roland Allen, *The Spontaneous Expansion of the Church* (Grand Rapids: Eerdmans, 1962),

98–99. This book was originally published in the 1920s.

2. Ibid.

3. Lawrence O. Richards and Clyde Hoeldtke, *A Theology of Church Leadership* (Grand Rapids: Zondervan, 1980), 60.

4. Edward A. White, "The Sunday-Monday Gap," *Faith Goes to Work,* comp. Robert J. Banks (Washington, D.C.: Alban Institute, 1993), 5.

5. Howard A. Snyder, *The Problem of Wineskins* (Downers Grove, Ill.: InterVarsity Press, 1975), 21.

Chapter 6: Freeing Spiritual Leaders to Lead

1. Ron Klassen and John Koessler, *No Little Places: The Untapped Potential of the Small-Town Church* (Grand Rapids: Baker, 1996), 99.

2. Eddy Hall and Gary Morsch, *The Lay Ministry Revolution* (Grand Rapids: Baker, 1995), 80–81.

3. Peter F. Drucker, "Time Management," *Leadership & Administration,* vol. 3 of *Leadership Handbooks of Practical Theology,* ed. James D. Berkeley (Grand Rapids: Baker, 1994), 79–80.

4. Klassen and Koessler, *No Little Places,* 99–100.

5. One of the clearest, most practical guides to how Jesus' training of the Twelve can serve as the pattern for leadership training in the church is Robert E. Coleman's *The Master Plan of Evangelism* (Grand Rapids: Revell, 1993).

Chapter 7: Putting Your Money Where Your Mission Statement Is

1. White, "The Sunday-Monday Gap," 4.

2. Howard A. Snyder, *A Kingdom Manifesto* (Downers Grove, Ill.: InterVarsity Press, 1985), 89–90.

3. Larry Woiwode, "A Conversation with Larry Woiwode," interview by Harold Fickett,

Image: A Journal of the Arts and Religion, 5 (spring 1994): 85.

Chapter 8: Growth Costs

1. I usually classify as "significant giving units" those giving units that gave five hundred dollars or more during the year and as "supporting giving units" those that gave less than five hundred dollars. I then propose a giving plan that depends primarily on the significant giving units. In McLane's case there were not enough significant giving units to develop a viable long-term giving plan; therefore I included all giving units that gave one hundred dollars or more.

2. As curriculum for the biblical financial principles class, I recommend *How to Manage Your Money: An In-Depth Bible Study on Personal Finances* by Larry Burkett (Chicago: Moody, 1991); for the spiritual gifts and personality class, I recommend *Personality Plus: How to Understand Others by Understanding Yourself* by Florence Littauer (Grand Rapids: Revell, 1992); and for the class on accepting your ministry, I recommend *The Lay Ministry Revolution: How You Can Join* by Eddy Hall and Gary Morsch (Grand Rapids: Baker, 1995).

Chapter 9: Something Worth Giving To

1. Klassen and Koessler, *No Little Places,* 35.

Chapter 10: Empowering People to Give

1. For an explanation of true debt, see page 48.

2. Josephus, *Antiquities of the Jews,* 4.4.3; 8.8.22.

3. The only New Testament references to tithing are either historical references to Old Testament events (Heb. 7:4–9) or references to Jewish worship (Matt. 23:23; Luke 11:42; 18:12).

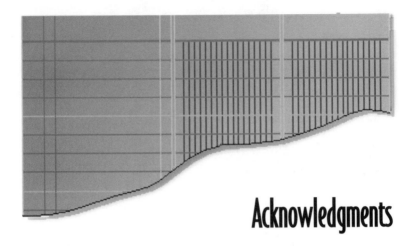

Acknowledgments

I am grateful to my wife, Sally, who willingly gave up much of her personal life to become an associate with me in our ministry of consulting. Replacing the comforts of home with living on the road is not easy. Her sensitivity to people and their needs and her gifts for analysis, critique, and encouragement have been vital to our effectiveness.

Since 1987 Eddy Hall has been our writer, organizing and interpreting our experiences for publication in professional journals for pastors and denominational magazines. In our writing this book, he not only continued in that role but also drew on his own study of Scripture, research, personal experience, and vision for

church renewal to contribute original material.

I want to thank James N. Posey who continues to encourage us to learn what the Bible teaches about finances and who provided office space for writing. Thanks to both James and Shirley for sharing their home and guest room with us.

Kent Davis, Pastor of Administration at Colorado Springs First Church of the Nazarene, opened the door that gave us the opportunity to do a major consultation for that church. Kent was invaluable to the writing of that story for this book and also read the entire manuscript and made helpful suggestions.

Thanks to Ralph and Sandy Turner for telling their story illustrating the application of biblical financial concepts in their personal life and in their church.

When Kim Hutchins was brought to us, he met our long-standing need for an associate in our consulting ministry. He has been prepared for this work with rich and varied experience as a lawyer; commercial real estate investor, developer, and broker; church builder; publisher and editor of *Mars Hill Review* (a journal exploring the intersection of Christianity and modern culture); and most important, a committed churchman and elder. As we have worked together he has strengthened and developed much of my material, especially in the area this book addresses—church finances.

He and I can be contacted at the following addresses:

LIVINGSTONE CONSULTING SERVICES
Strategic Planning for the Growing Church
Finances • Facilities • Staffing • Ministry

Kim Hutchins
11757 W. Ken Caryl F330
Littleton, CO 80127-3700
(303) 697-0195

Ray Bowman
4526 Sentinel Rock Terrace
Larkspur, CO 80118-8905
(303) 681-3543